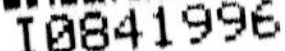

I0841996

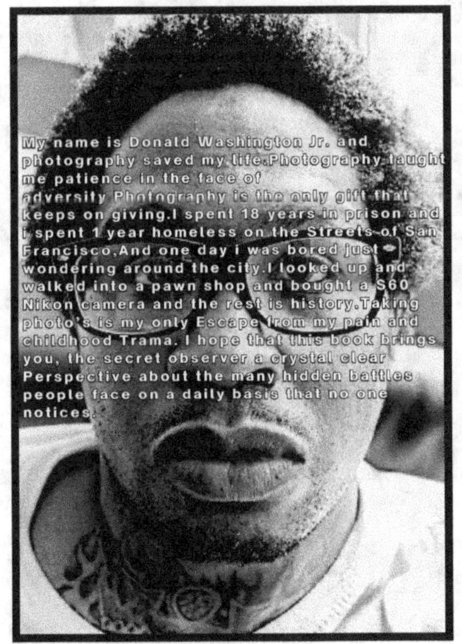

My name is Donald Washington Jr. and photography saved my life.Photography taught me patience in the face of adversity.Photography is the only gift that keeps on giving.I spent 18 years in prison and i spent 1 year homeless on the Streets of San Francisco.And one day i was bored just wondering around the city.I looked up and walked into a pawn shop and bought a S60 Nikon camera and the rest is history.Taking photo's is my only Escape from my pain and childhood Trama. I hope that this book brings you, the secret observer a crystal clear Perspective about the many hidden battles people face on a daily basis that no one notices.

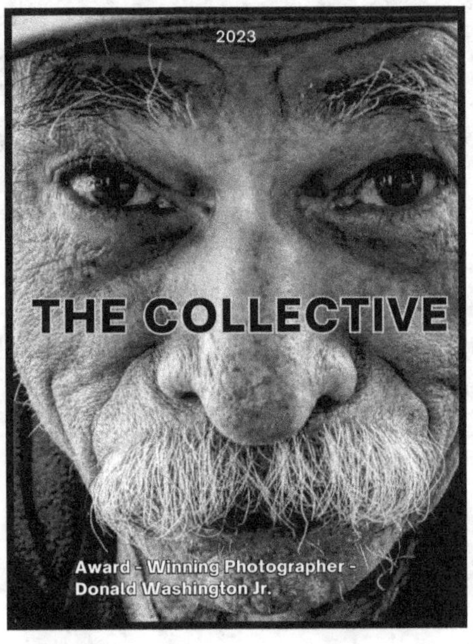

2023
THE COLLECTIVE
Award - Winning Photographer - Donald Washington Jr.

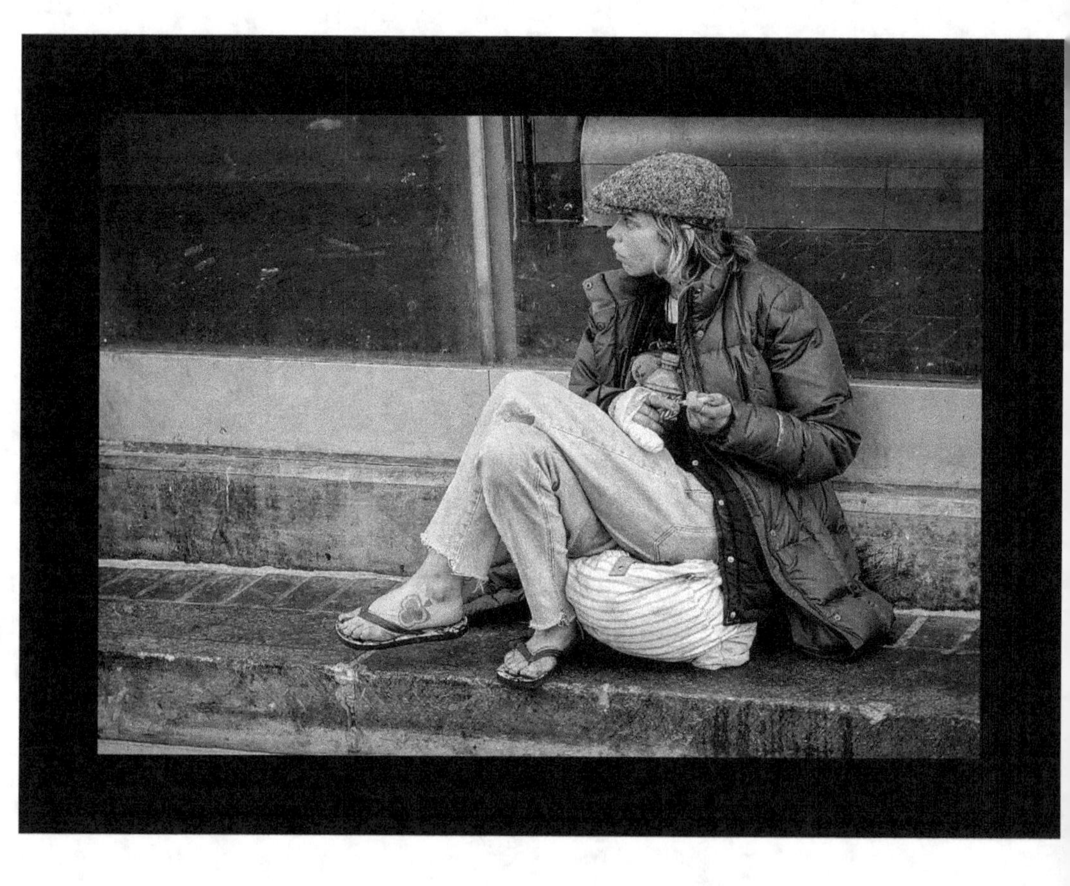

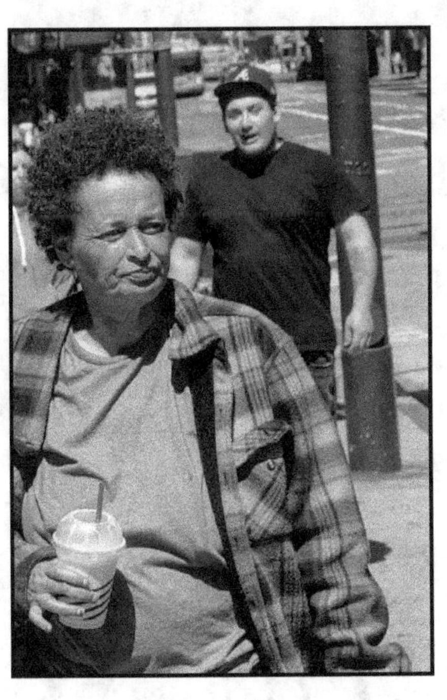

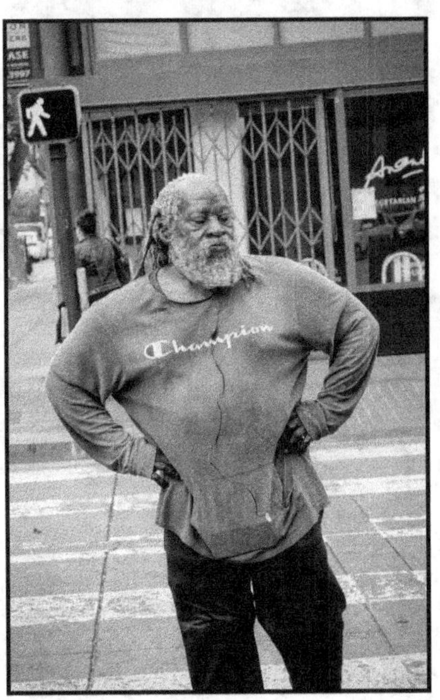

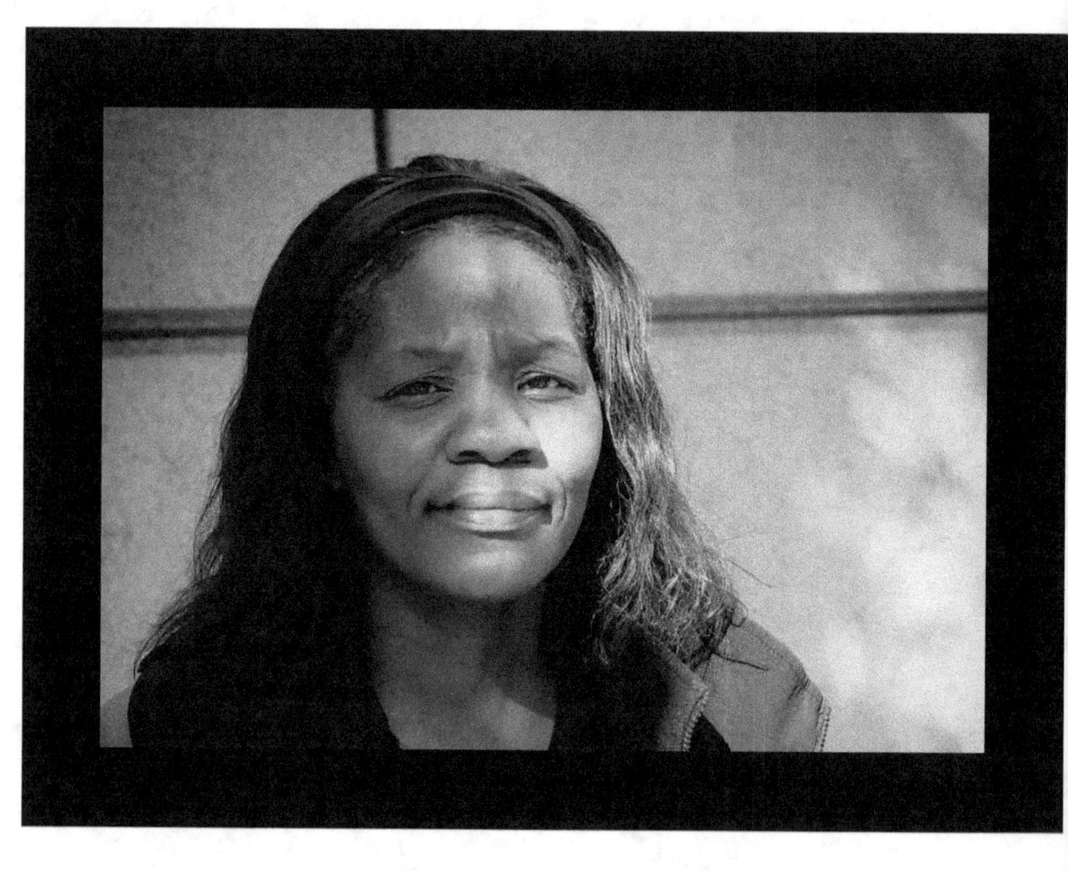

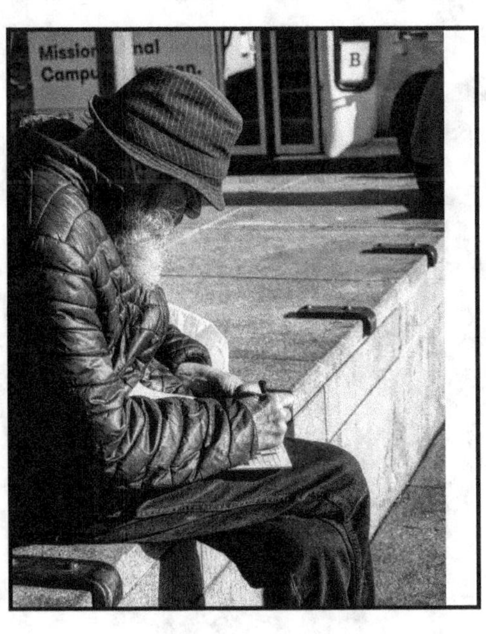
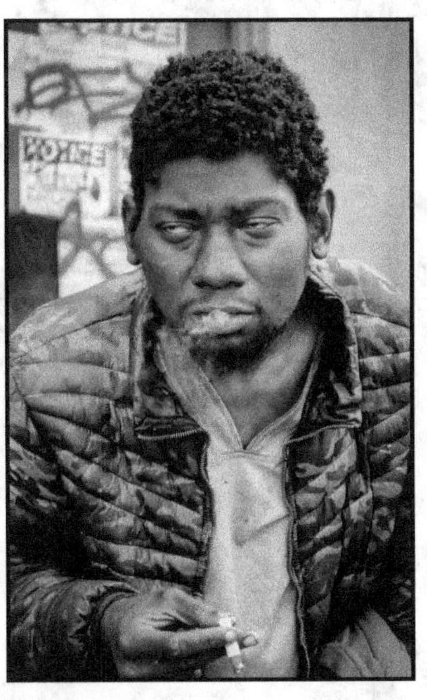

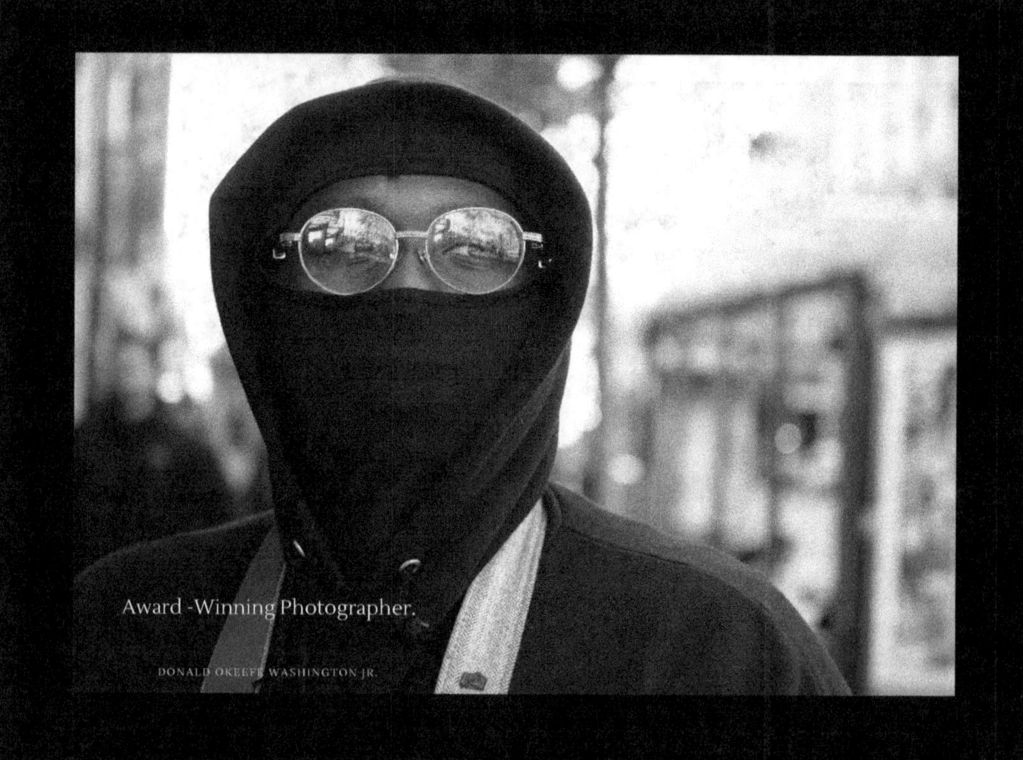
Award -Winning Photographer.
DONALD OKEEFE WASHINGTON JR.

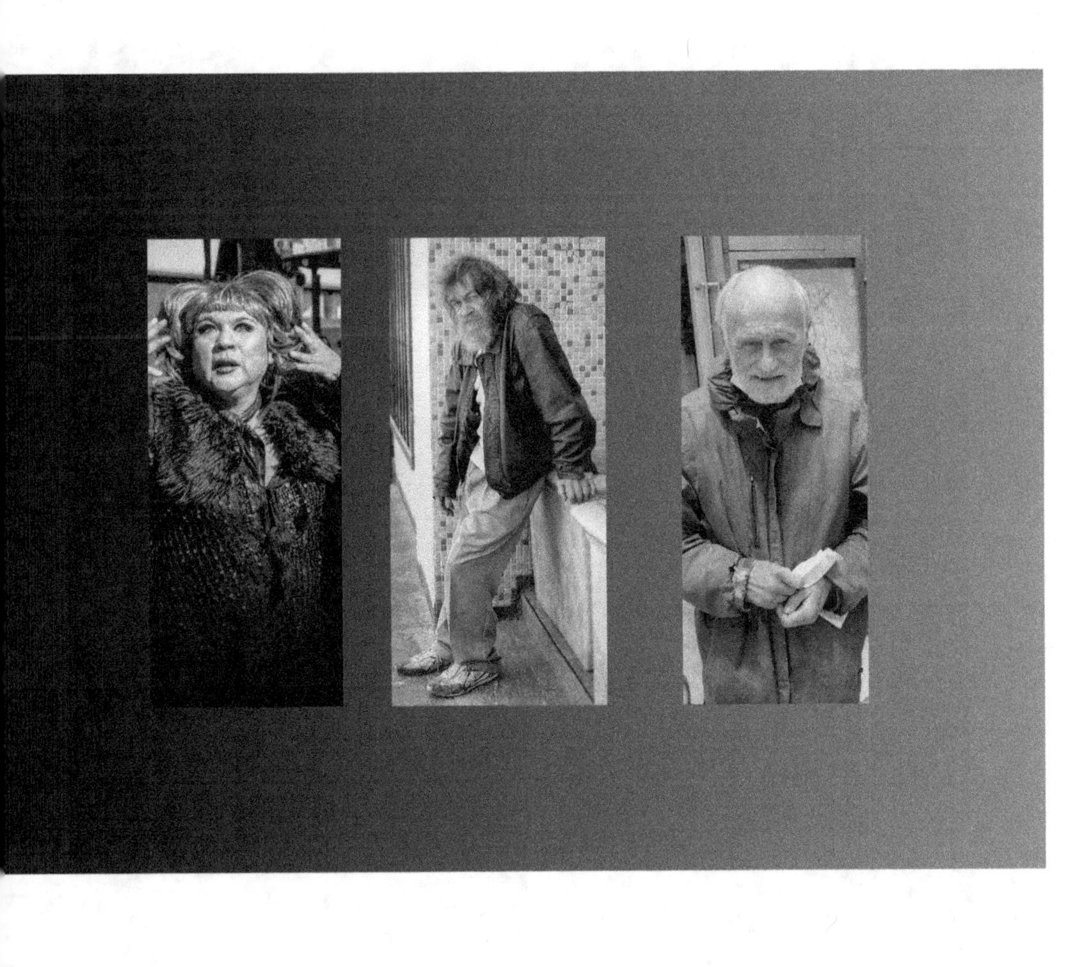

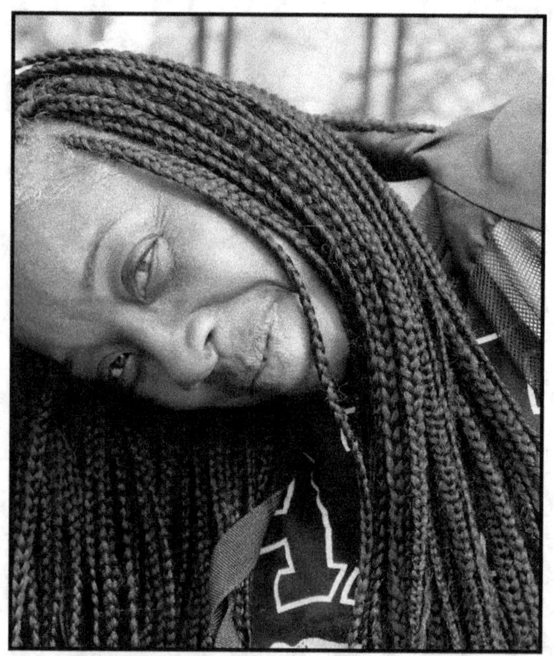

People move fast. It presents a wonderful opportunity to capture life as it flows day in and day out.

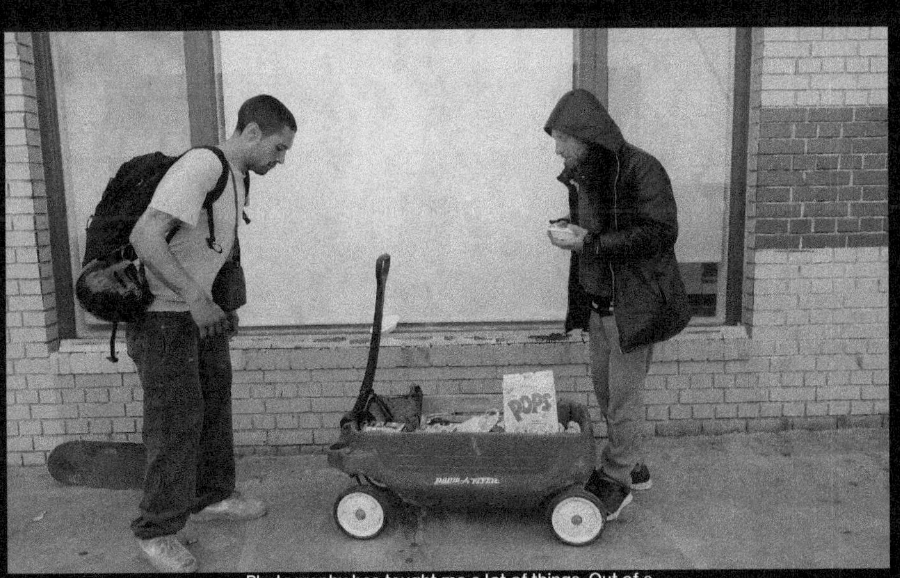

Photography has taught me a lot of things. Out of a hundred,
one stands out and that is life is all about perspective.

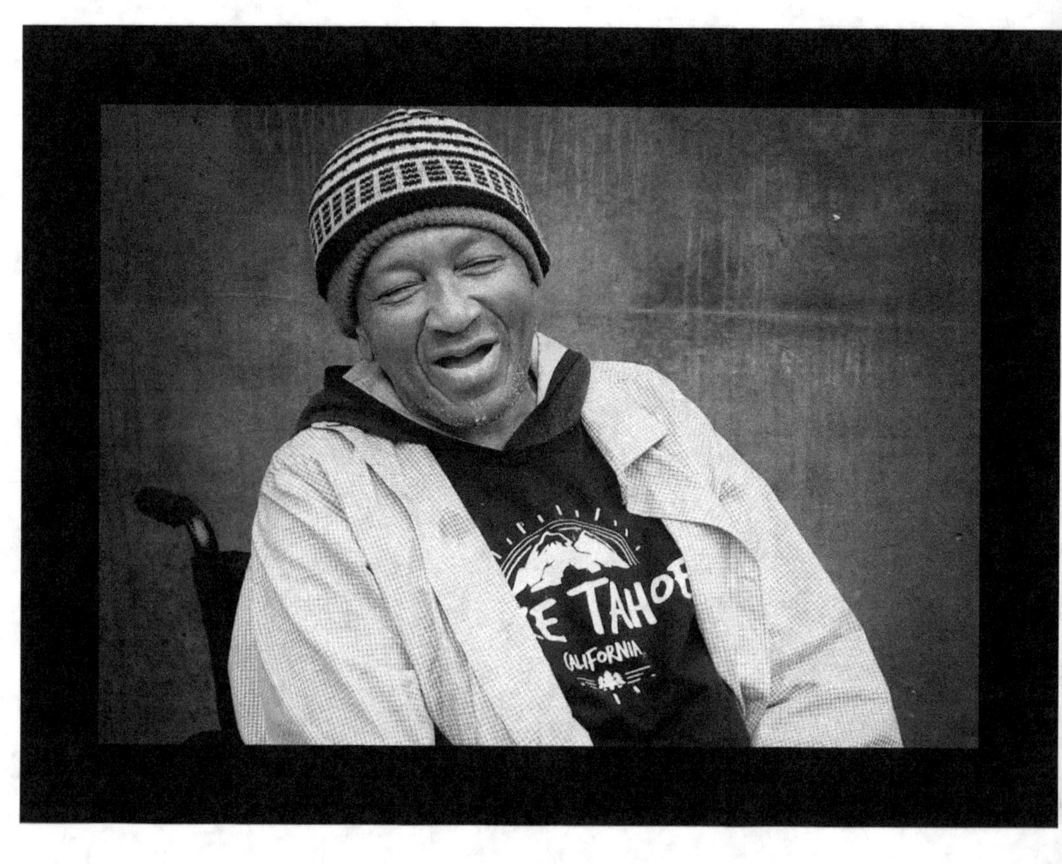
E TAHOE
CALIFORNIA

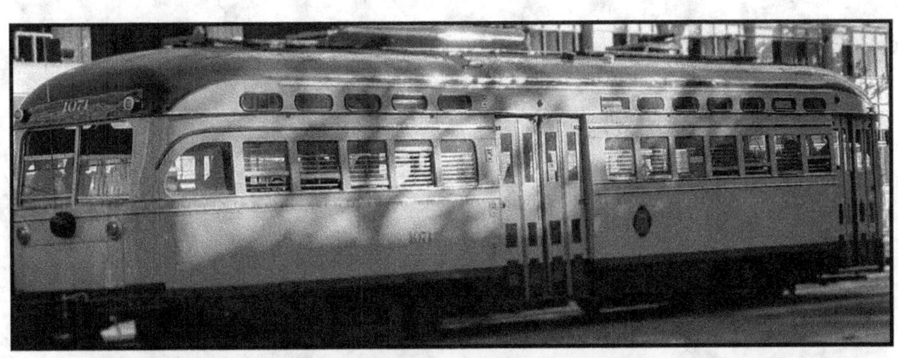
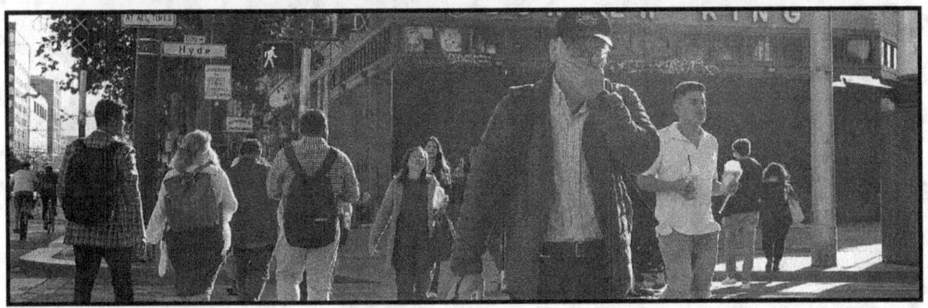
AT ALL TIPES
Hyde

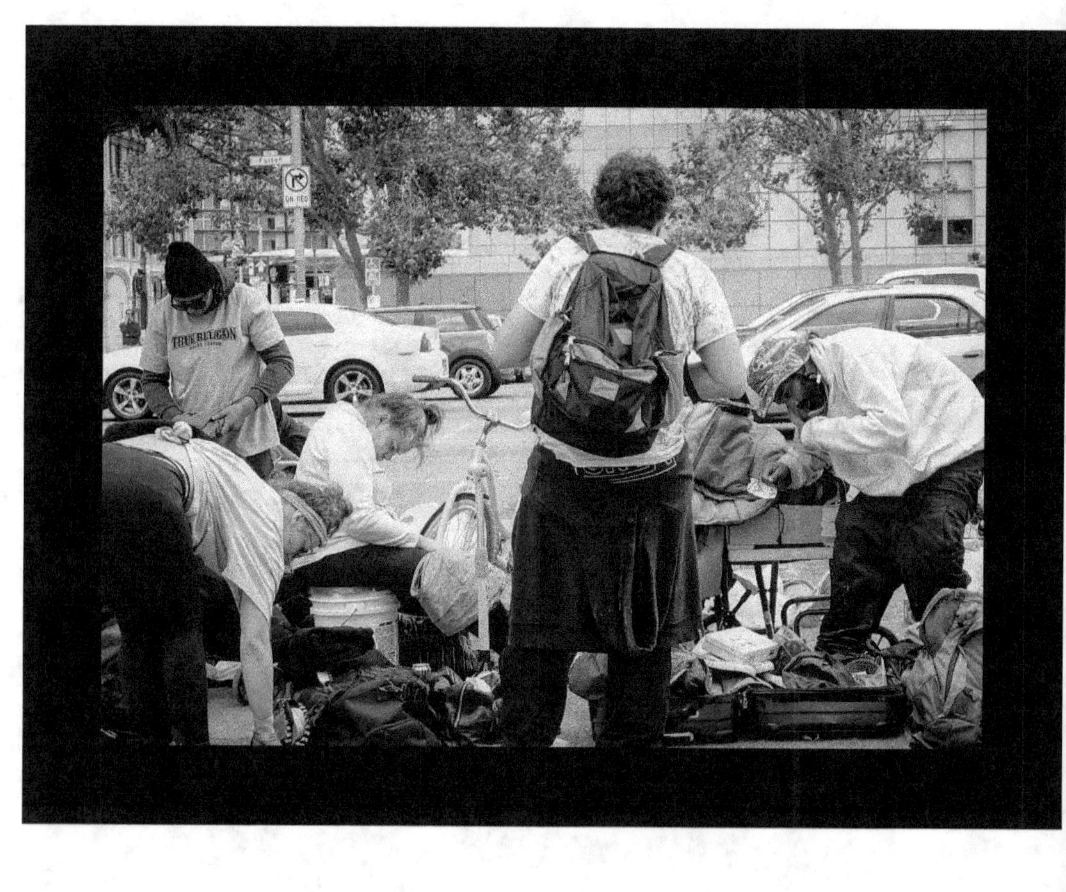

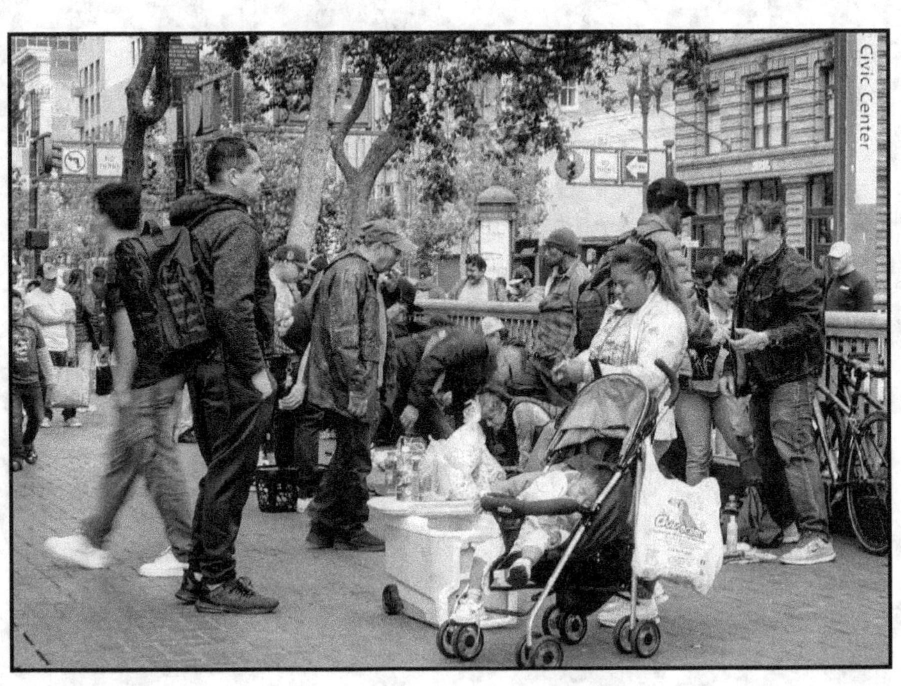
Civic Center

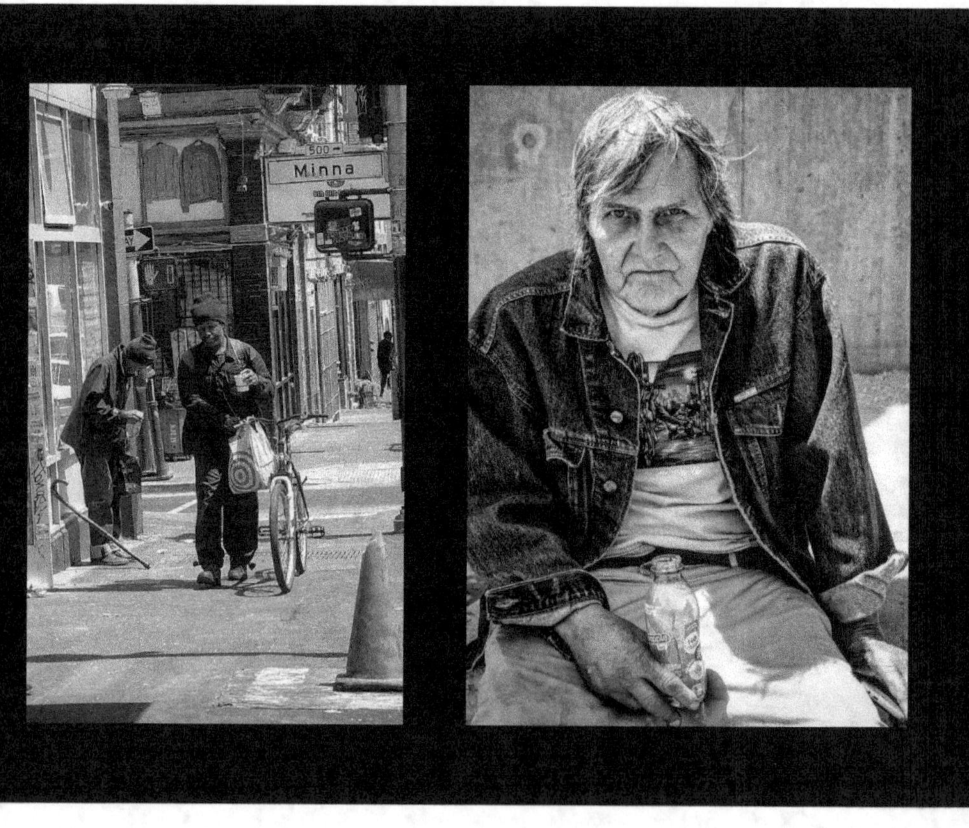

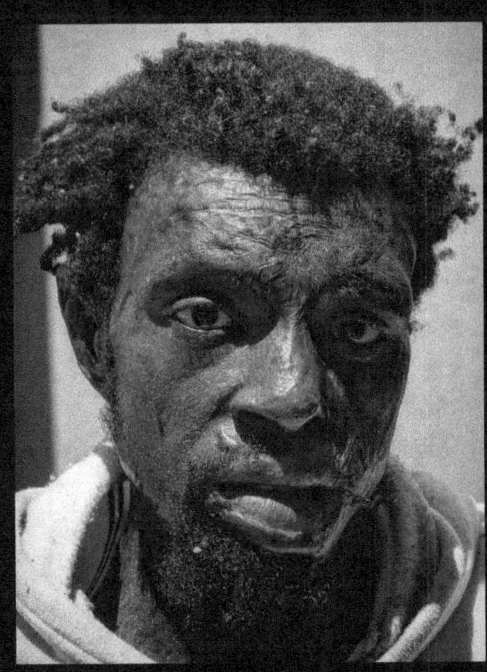

It's all in the eyes. *How do you look at the world around you?* As a photographer, this is what I've learned to ask myself, again and again.

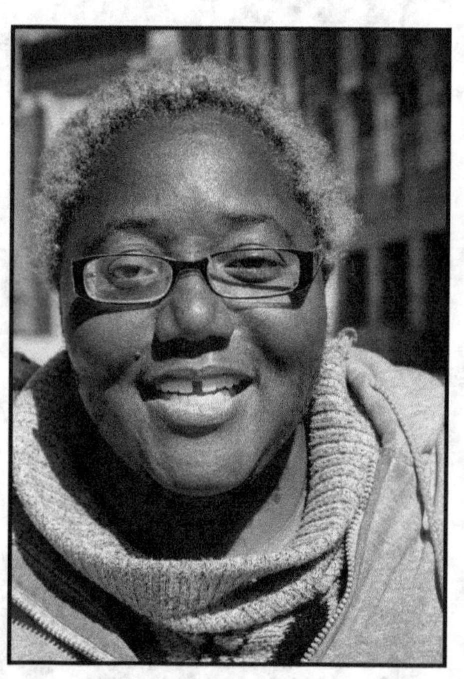 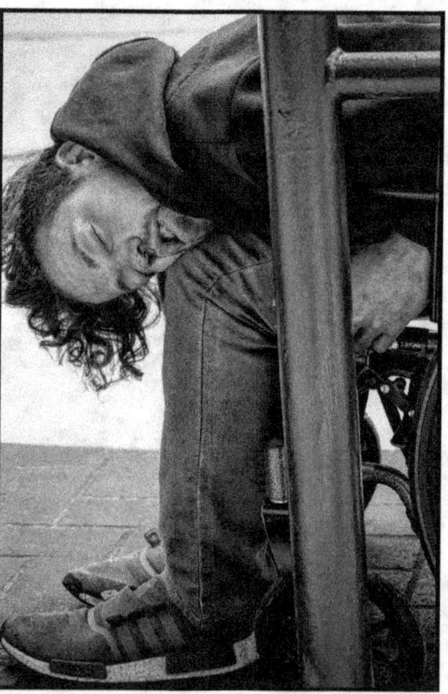

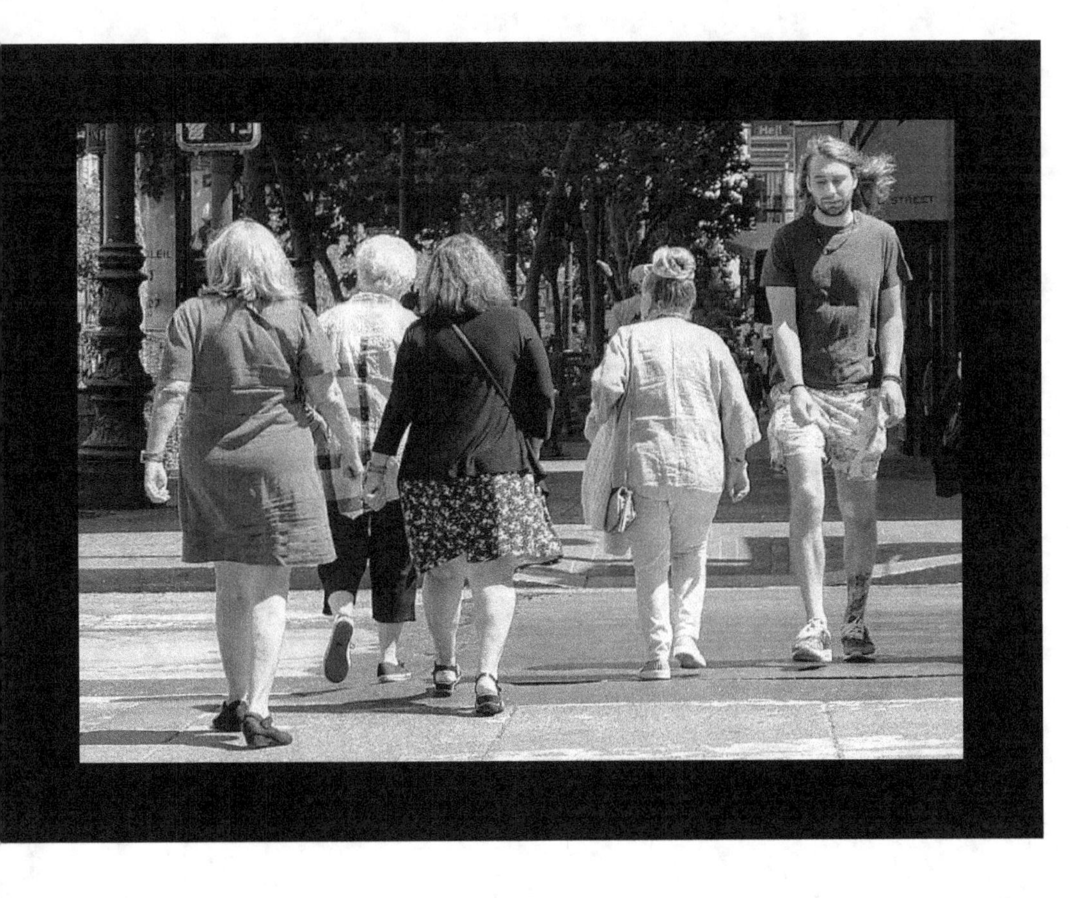

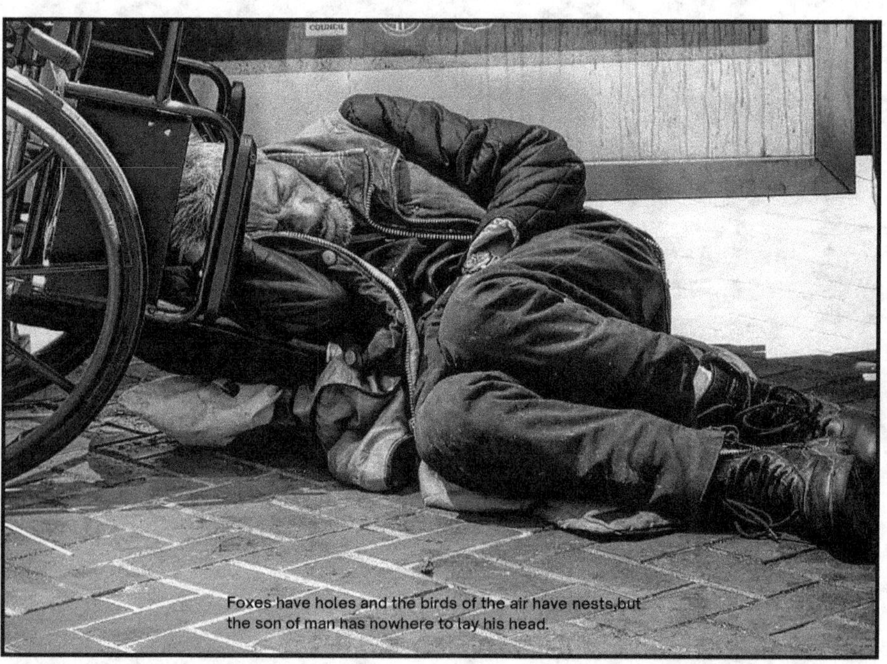

Foxes have holes and the birds of the air have nests,but
the son of man has nowhere to lay his head.

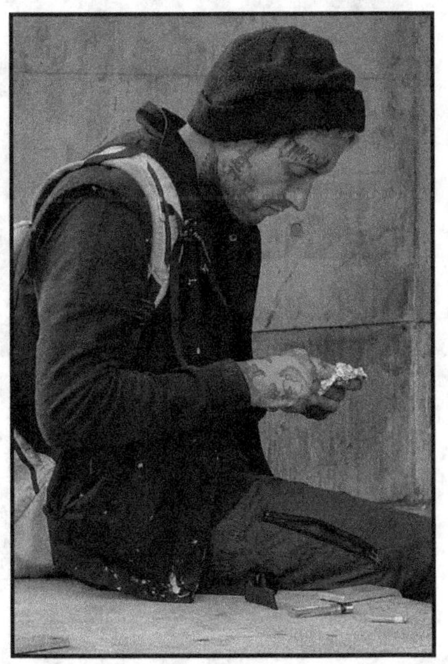

Light and darkness change the way we see.

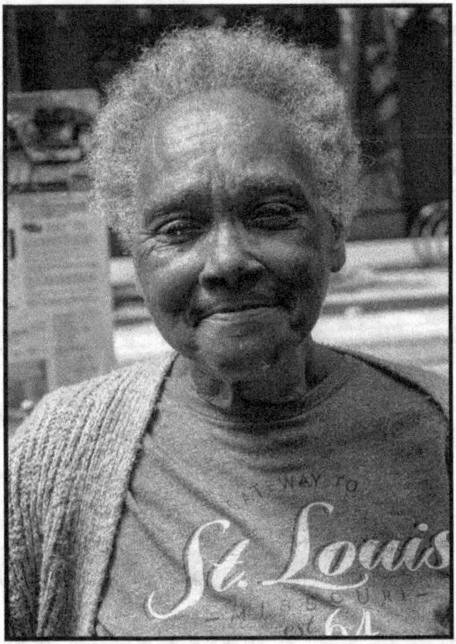

WAY TO
St. Louis
MISSOURI
est 64

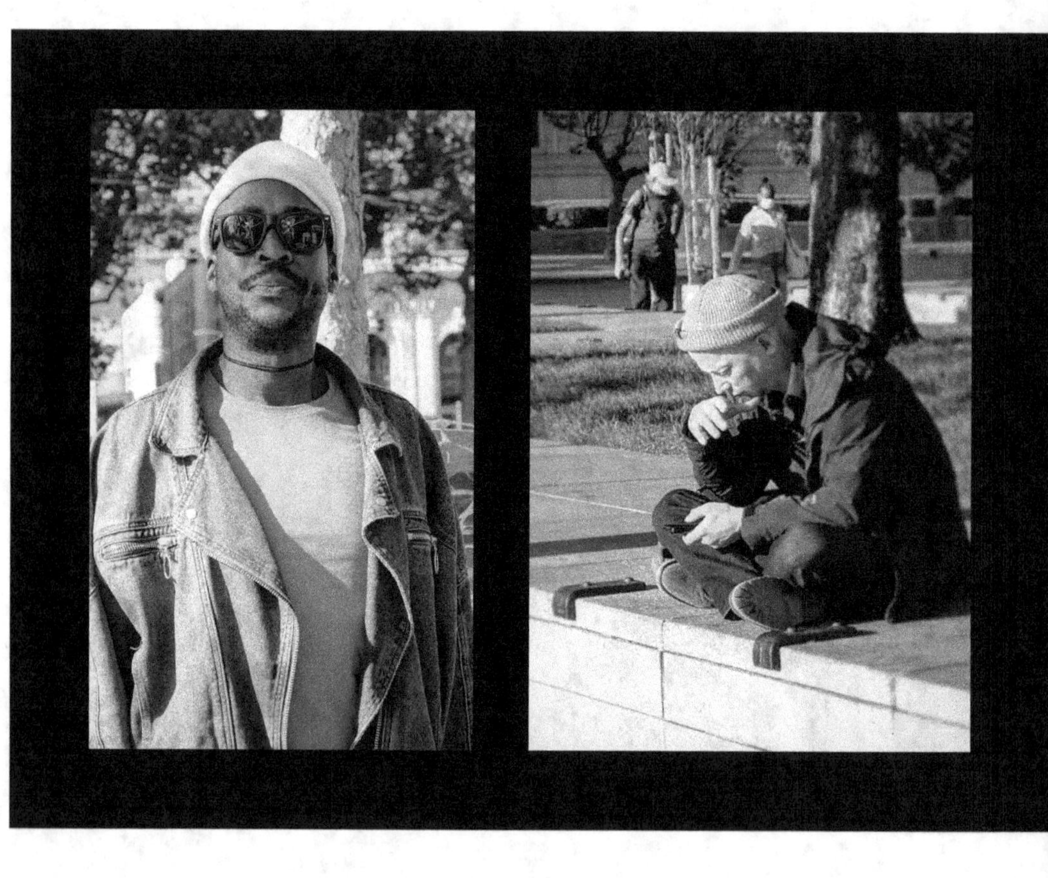

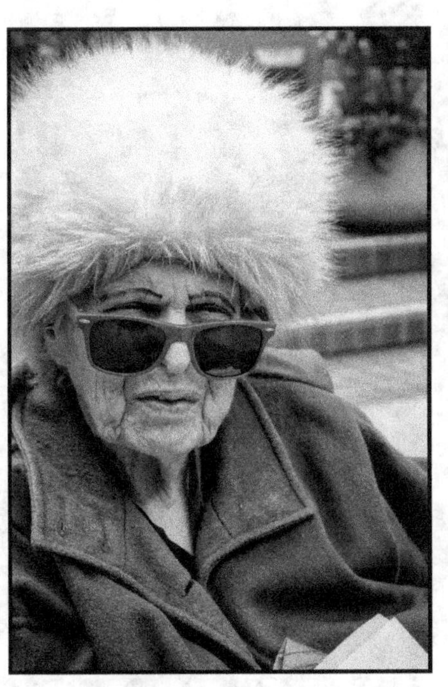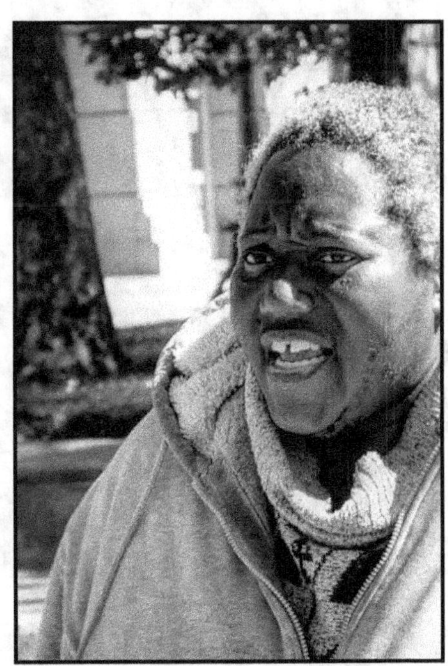

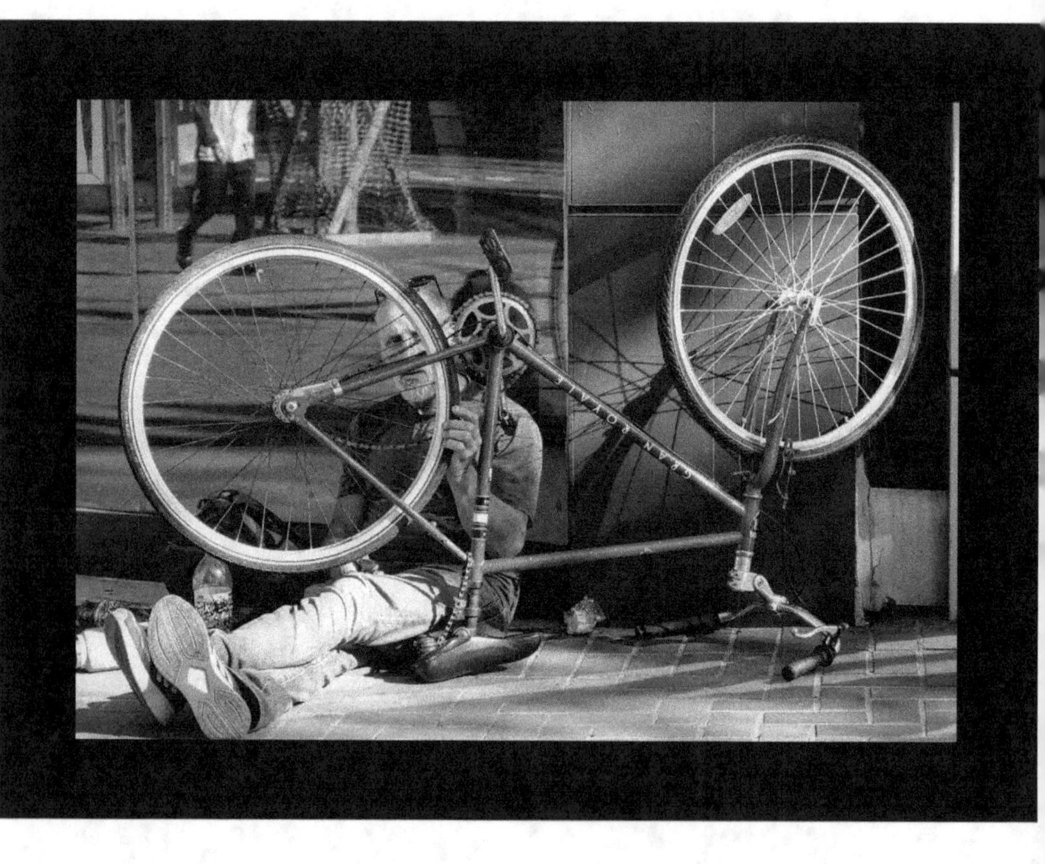

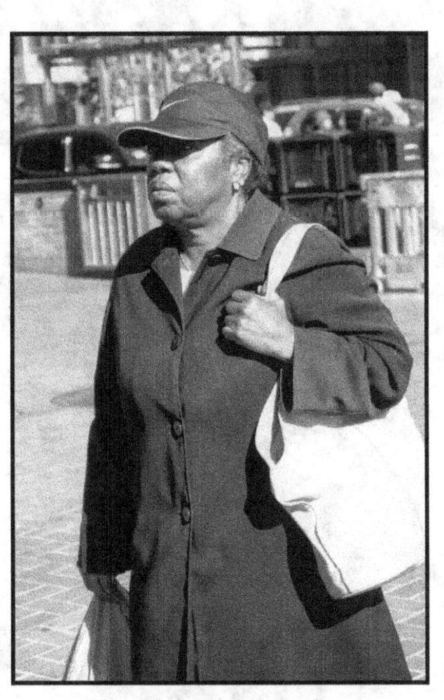 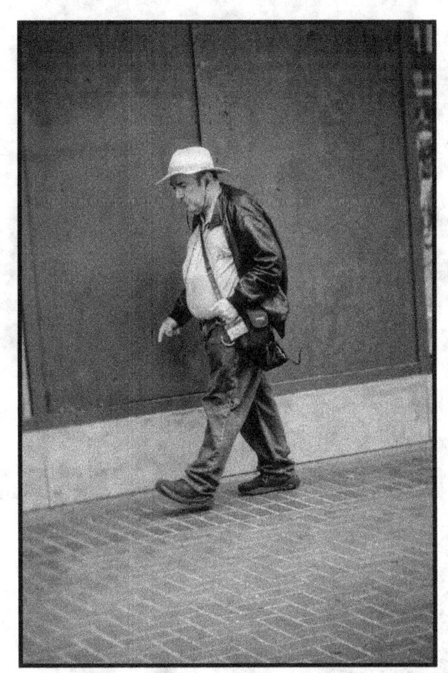

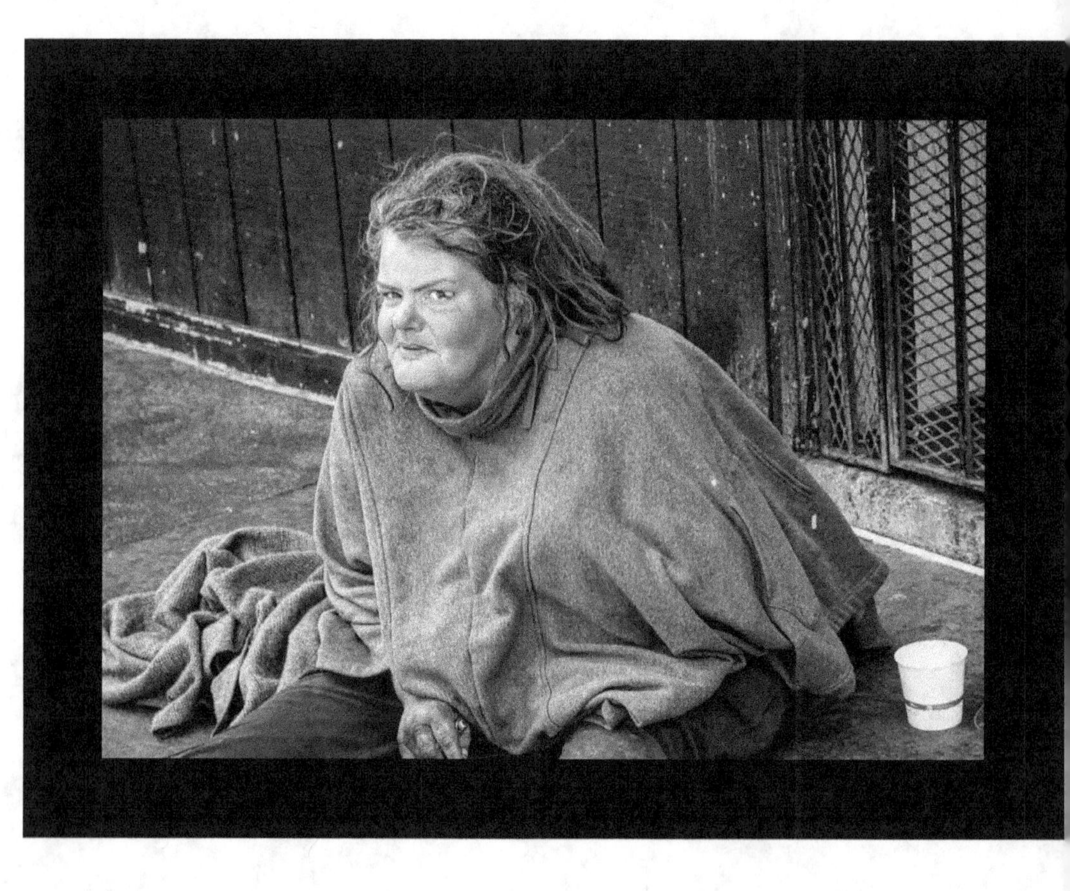

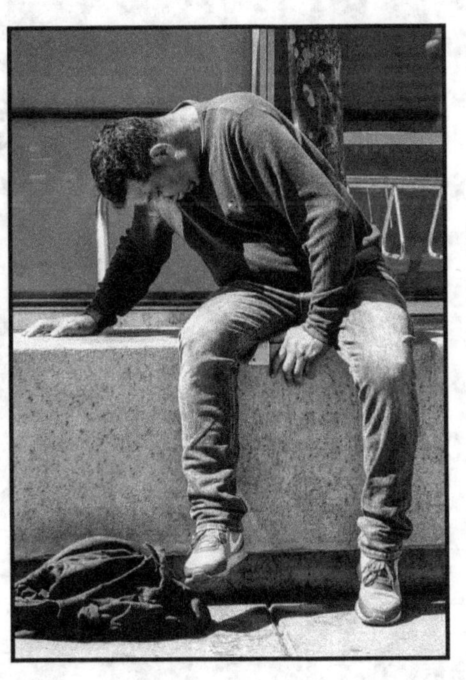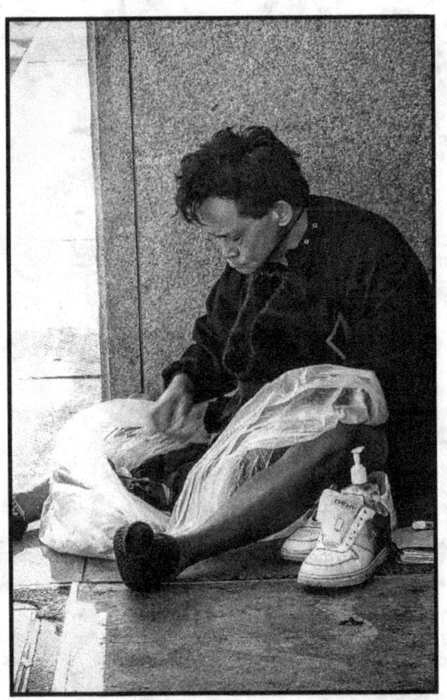

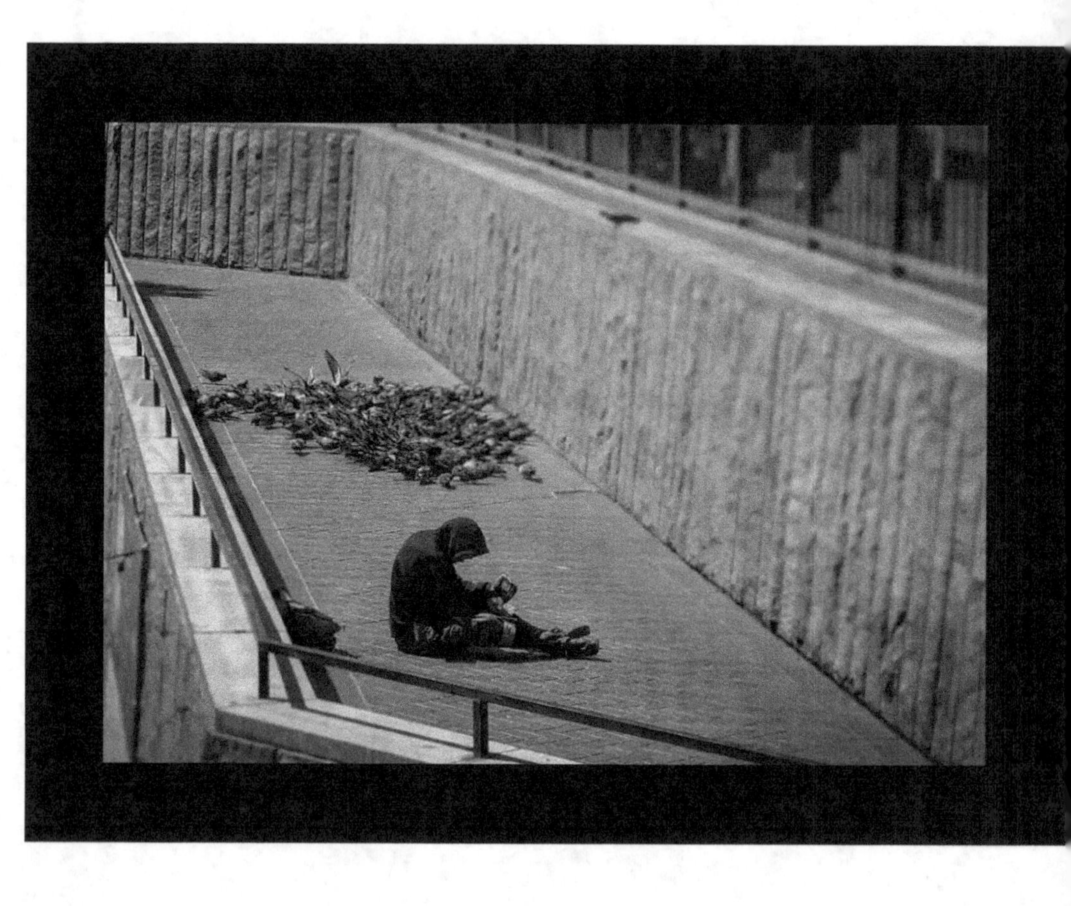

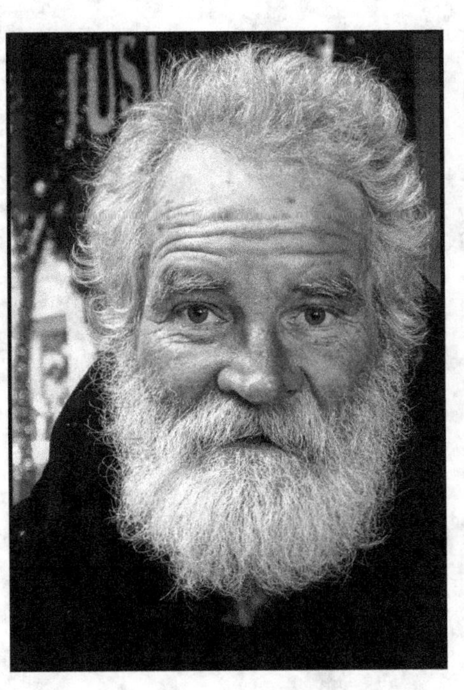
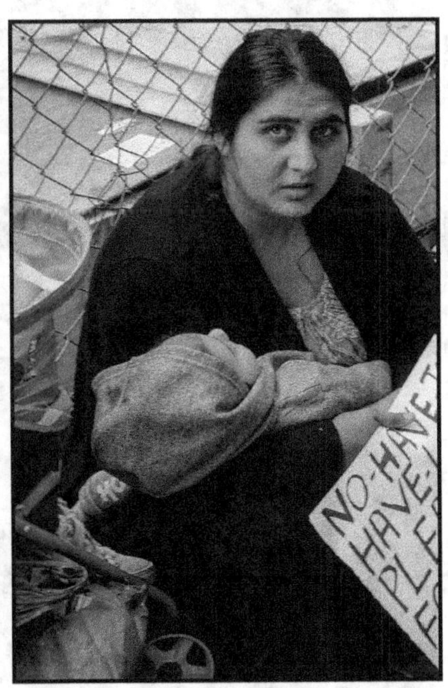
NO-HAVE
HAVE
PLEA

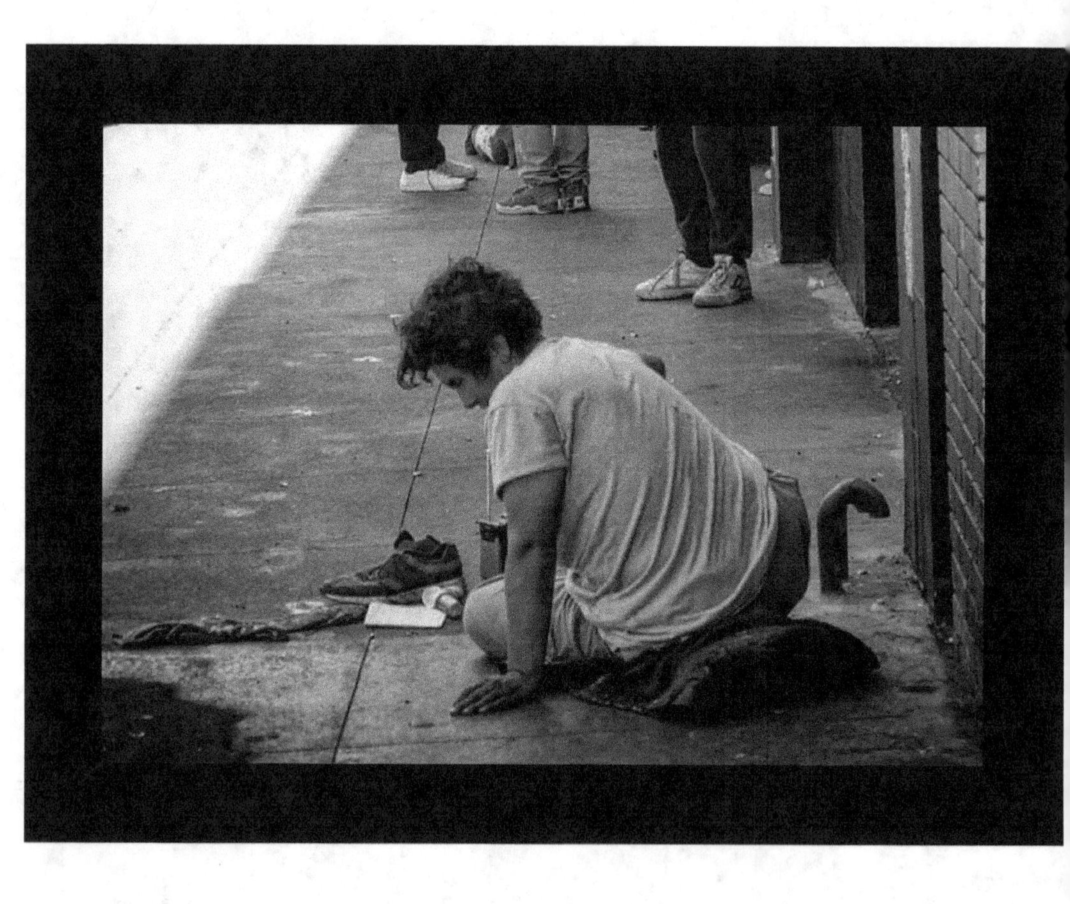

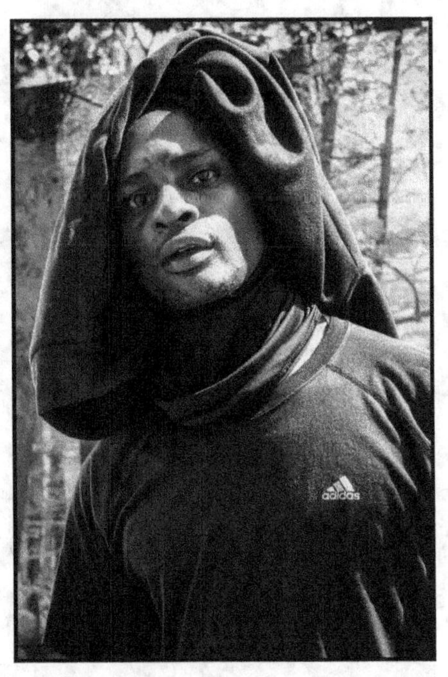 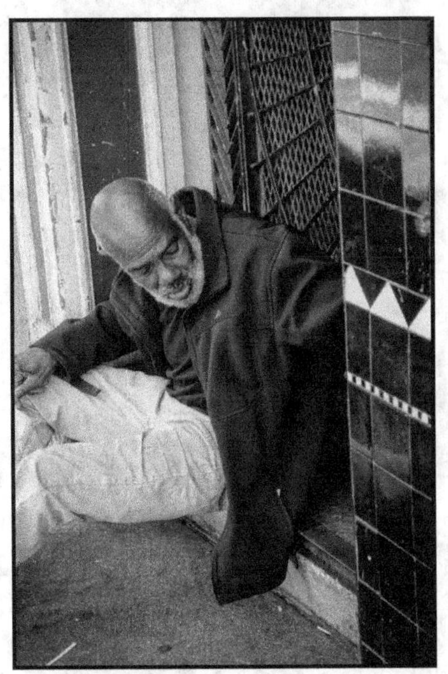

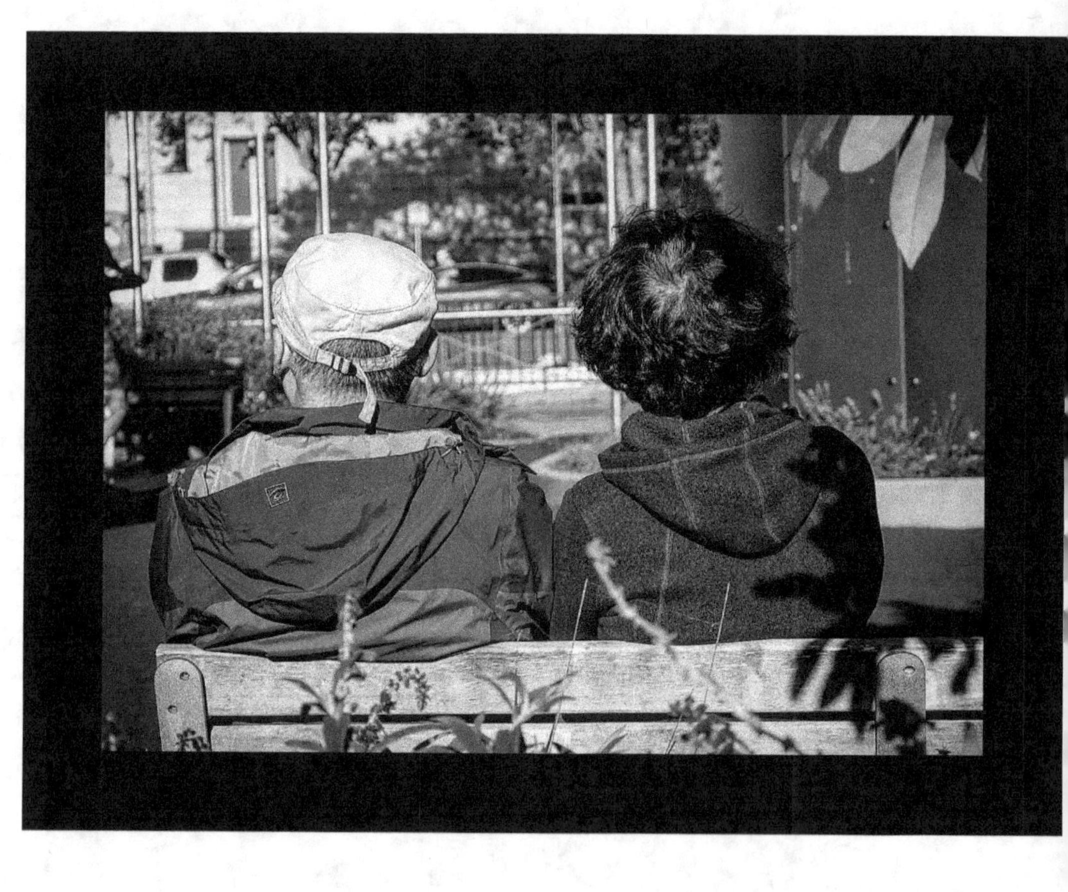

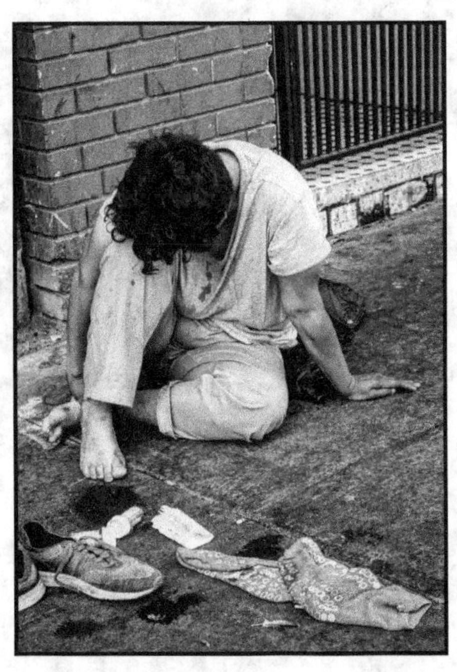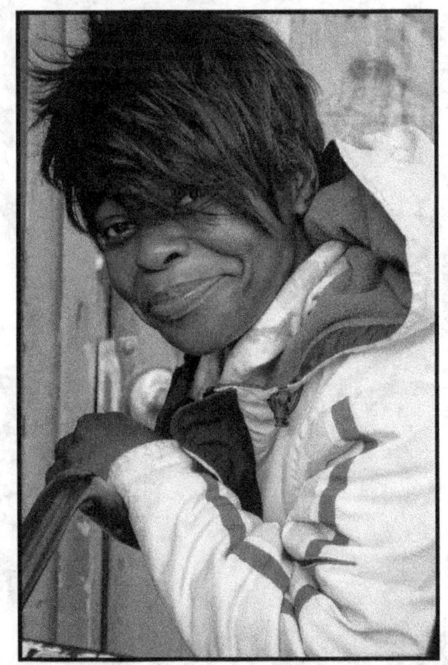

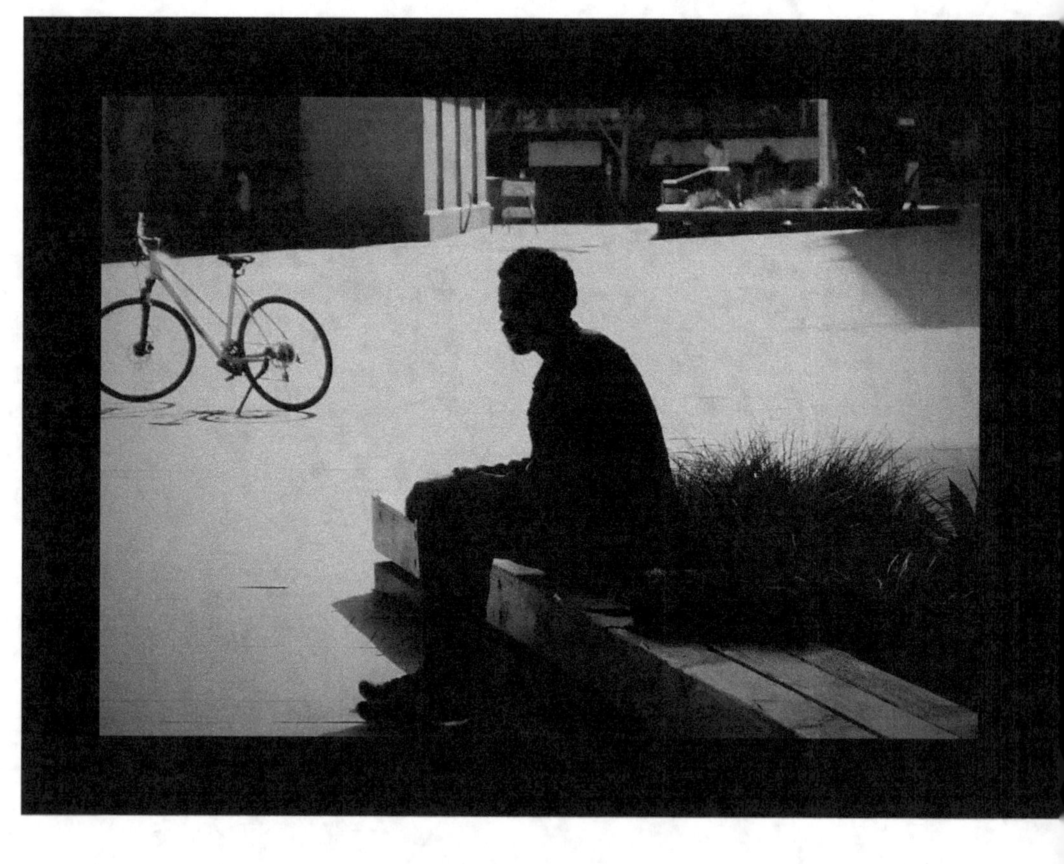

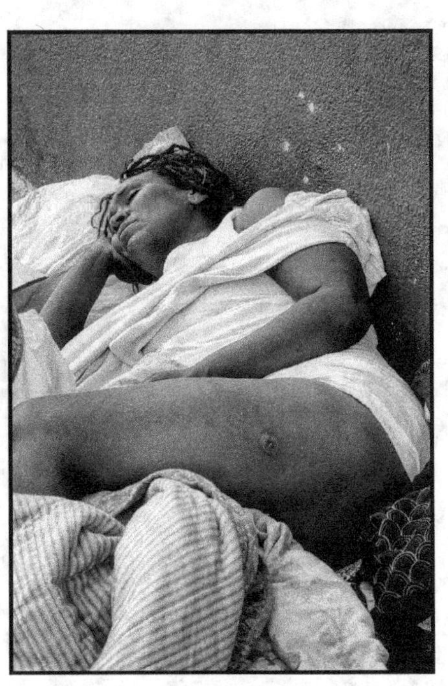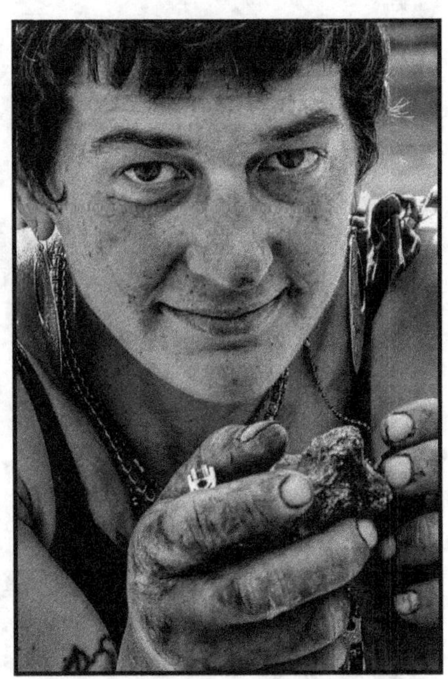

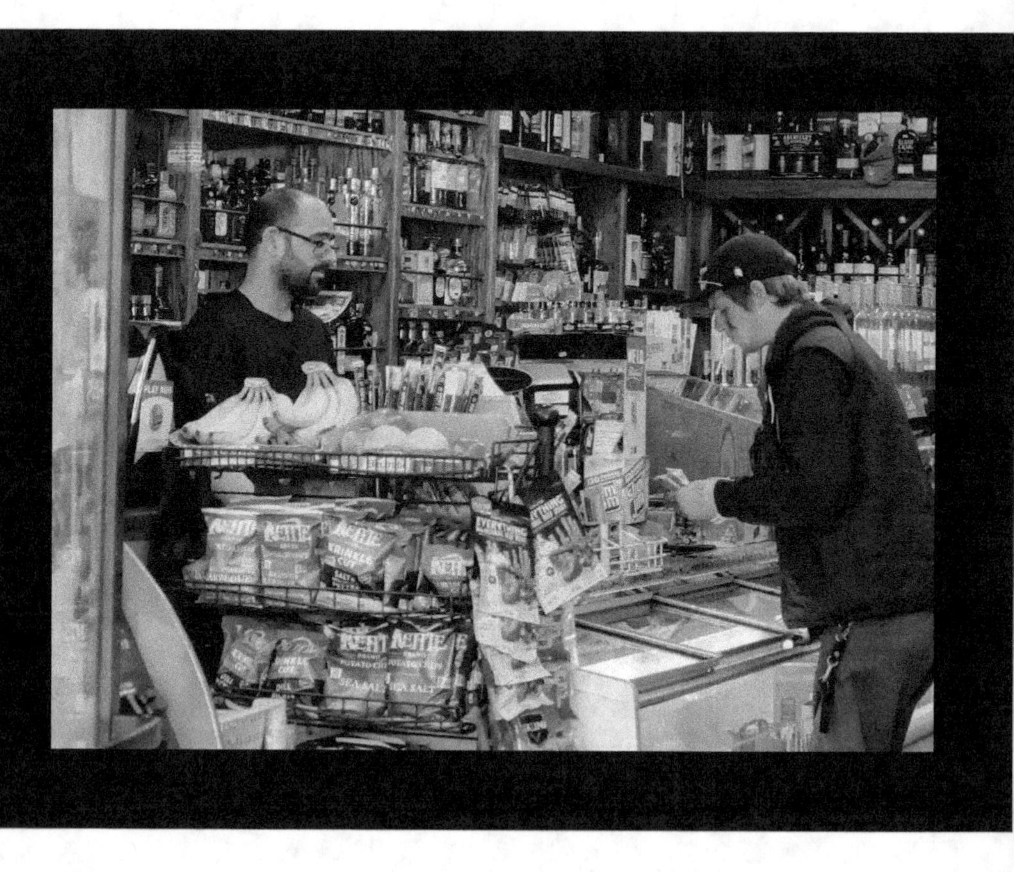

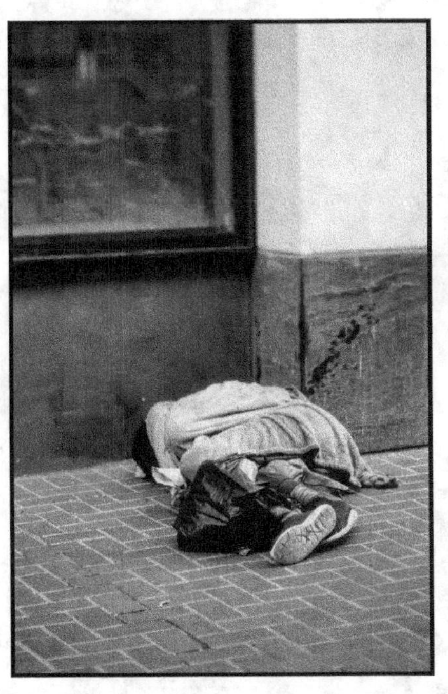
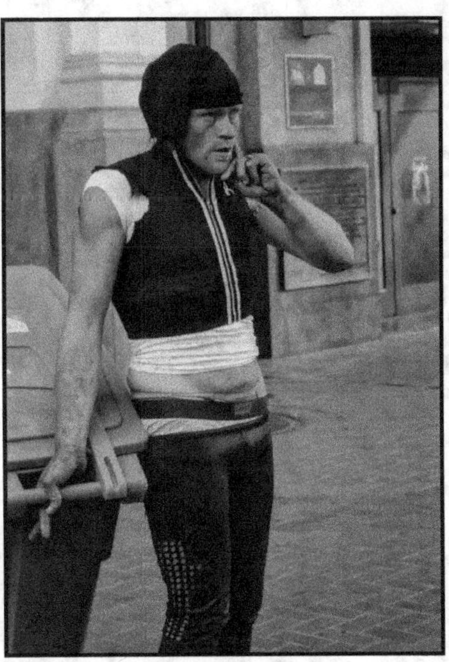

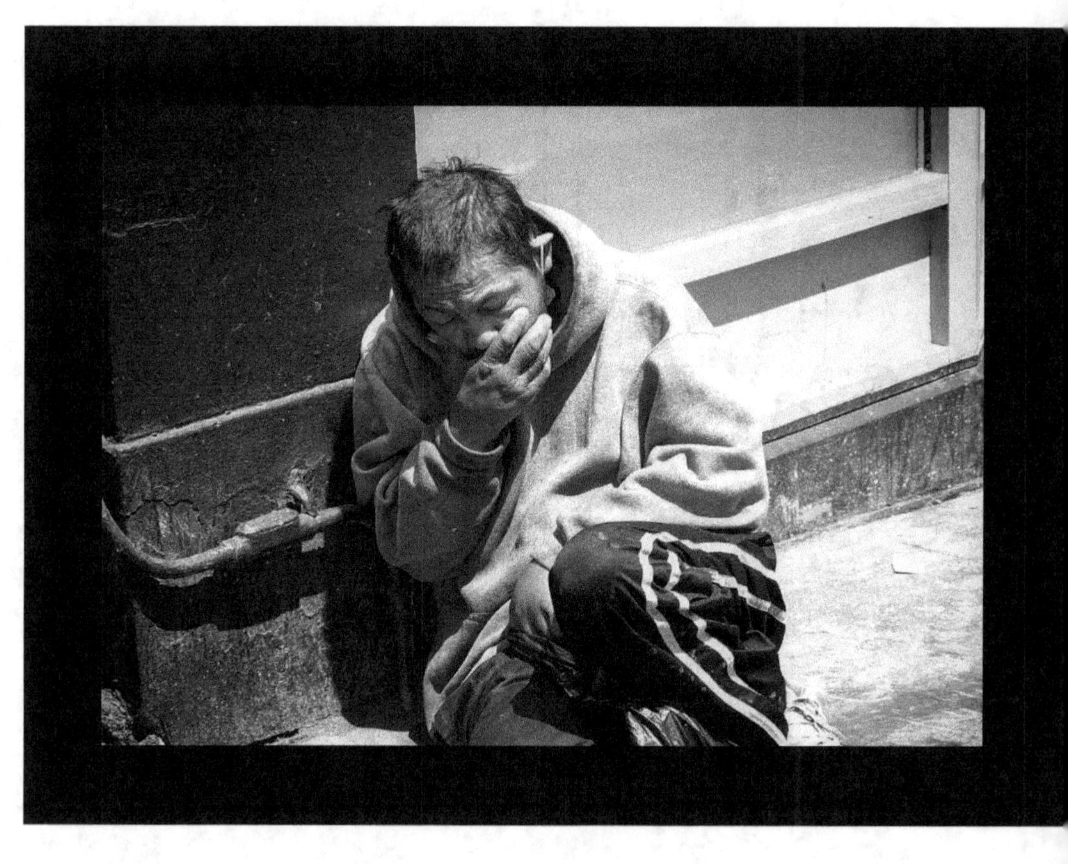

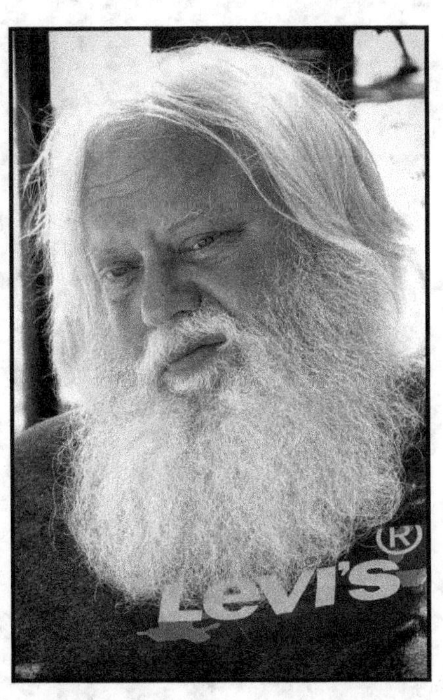

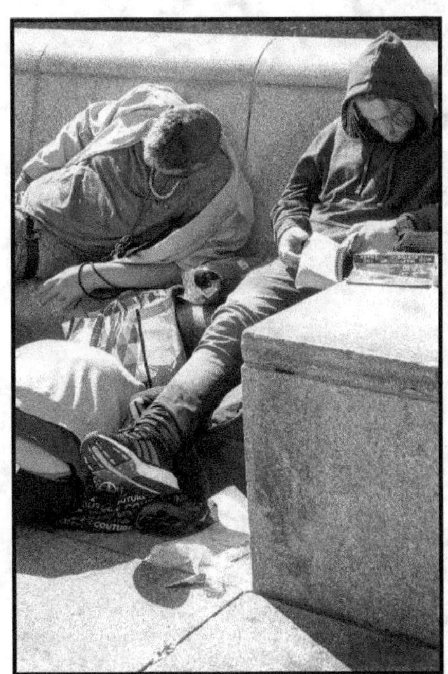

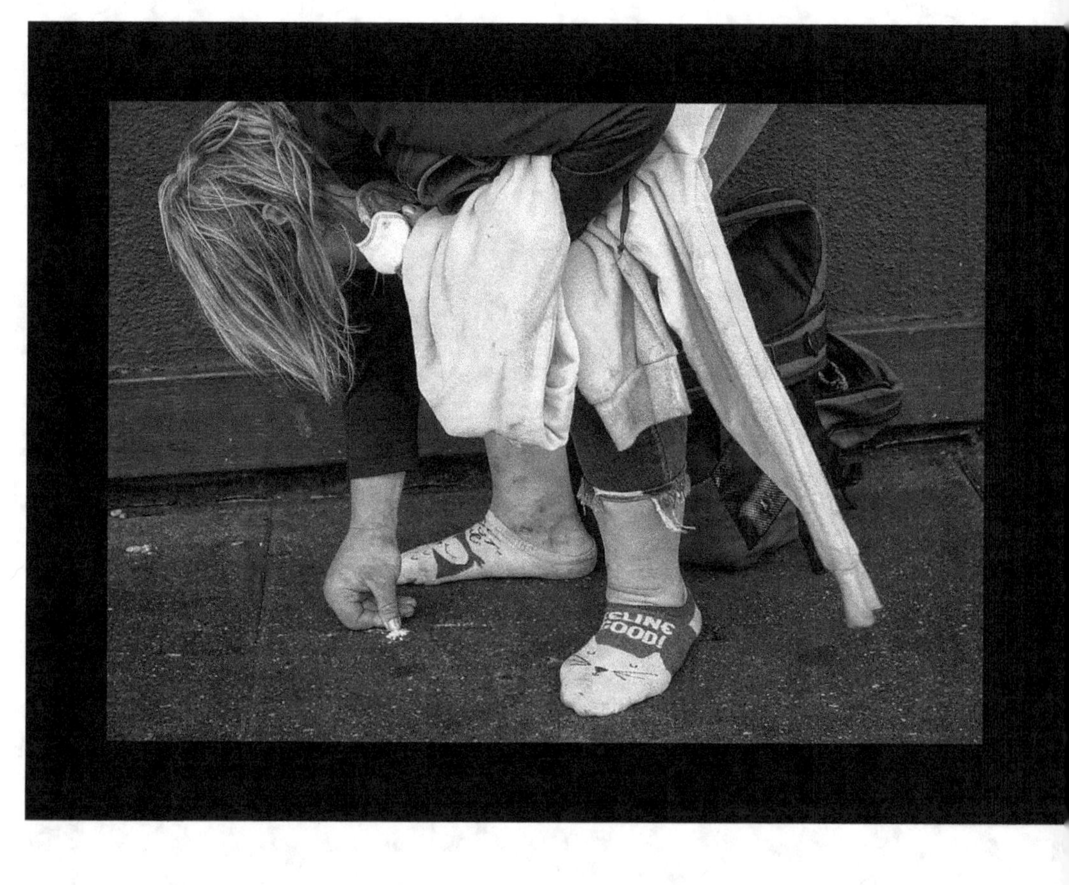

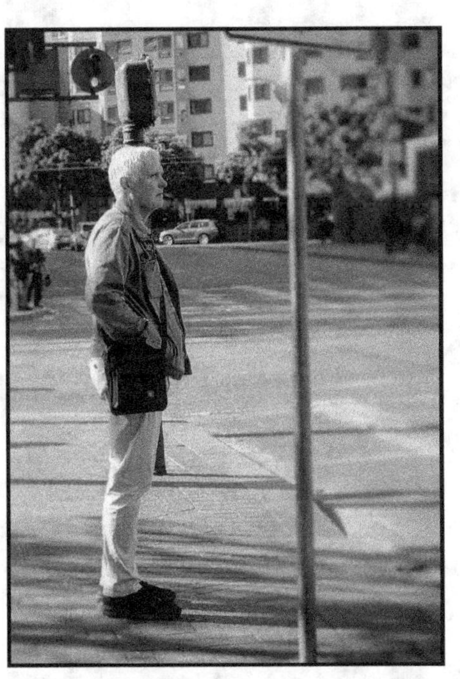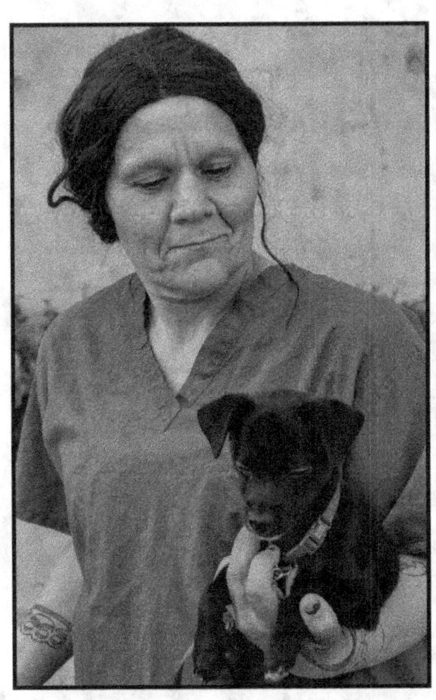

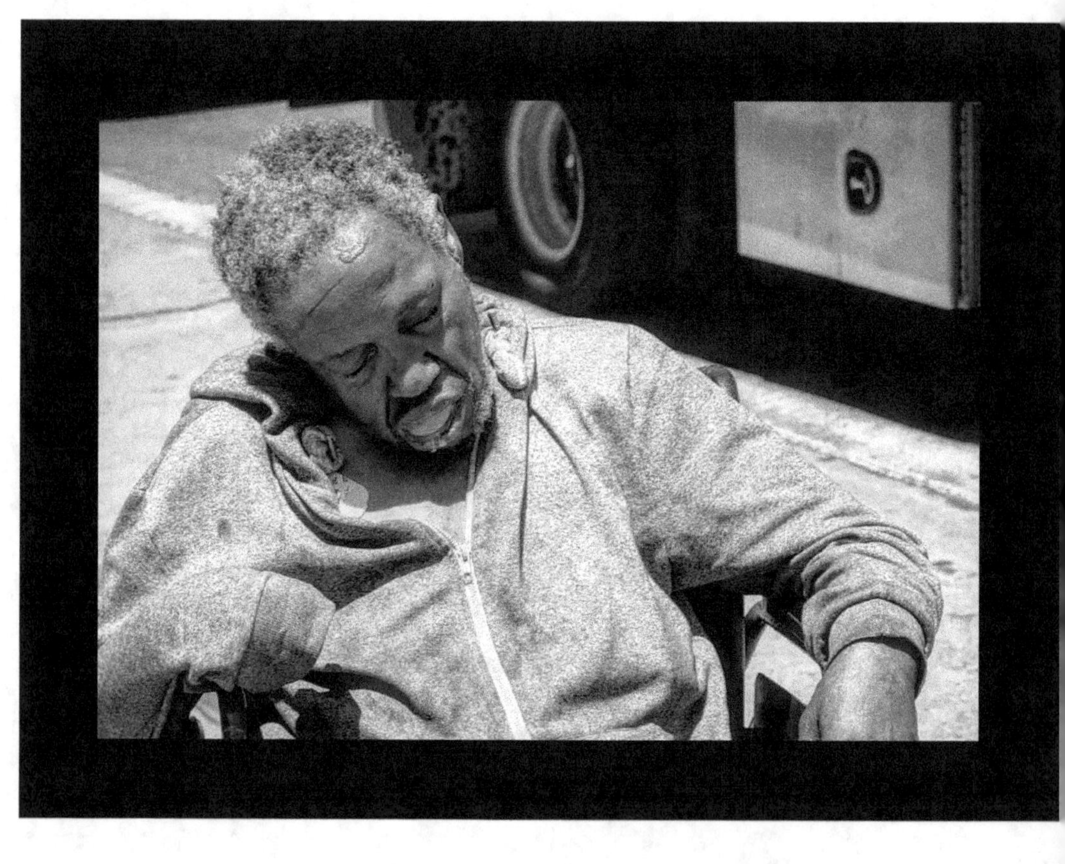

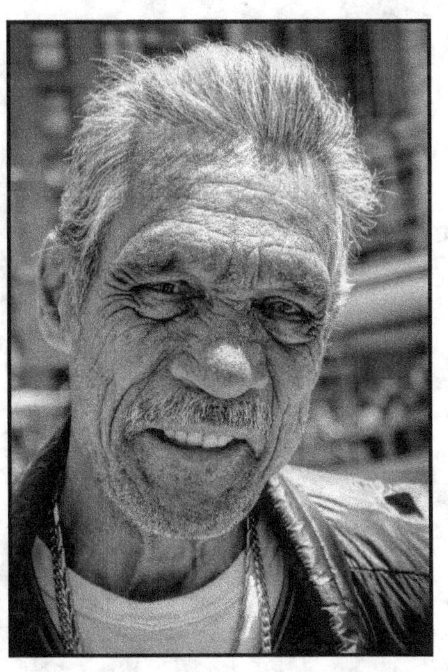
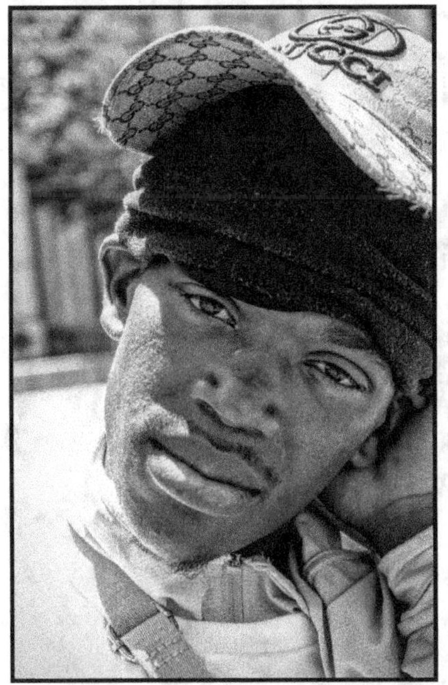

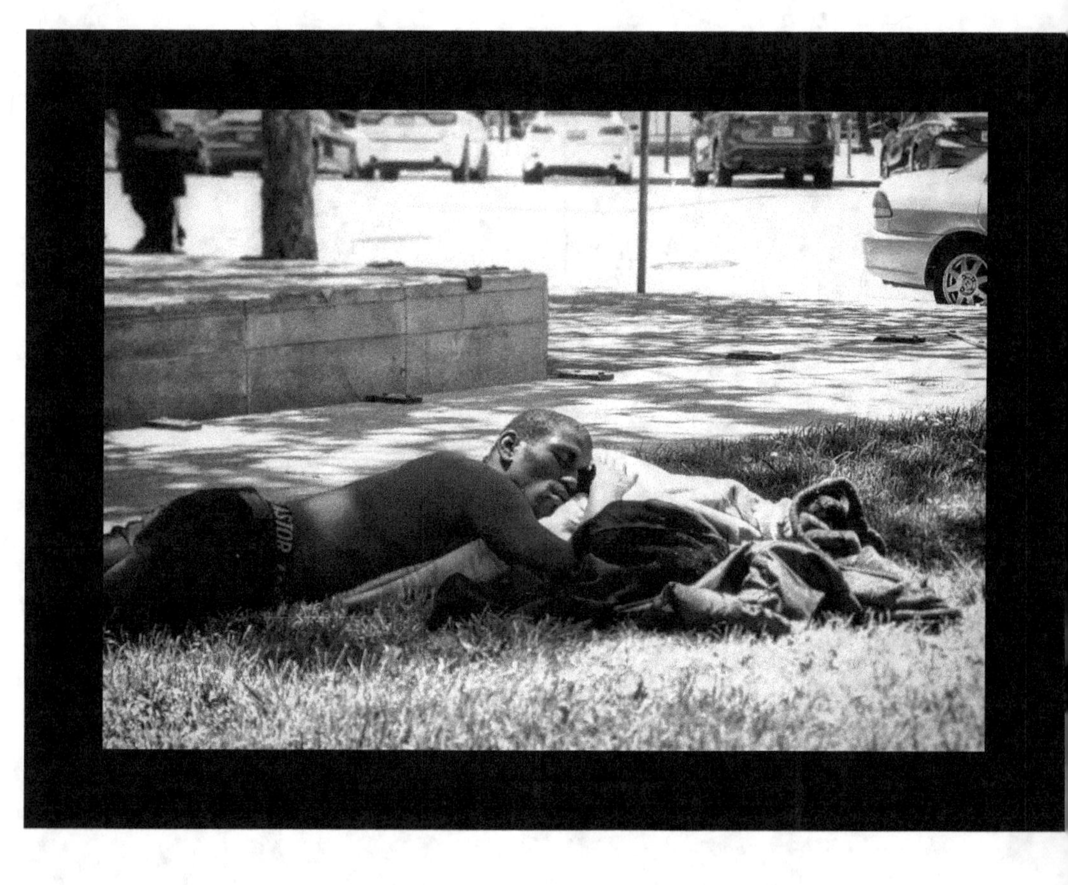

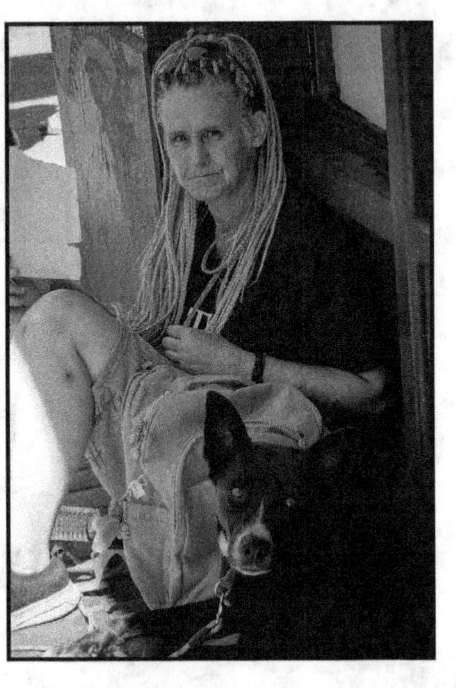
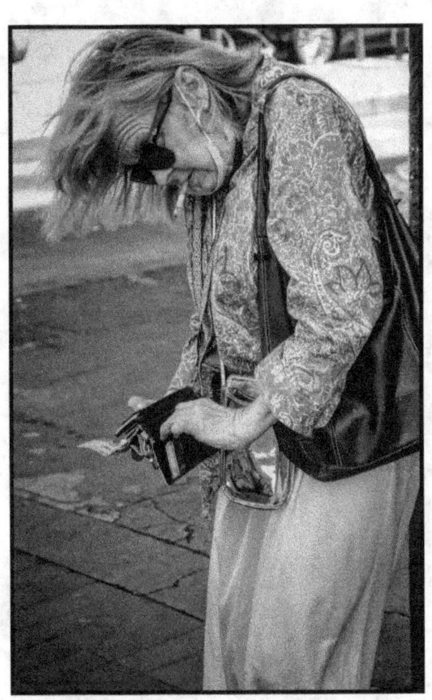

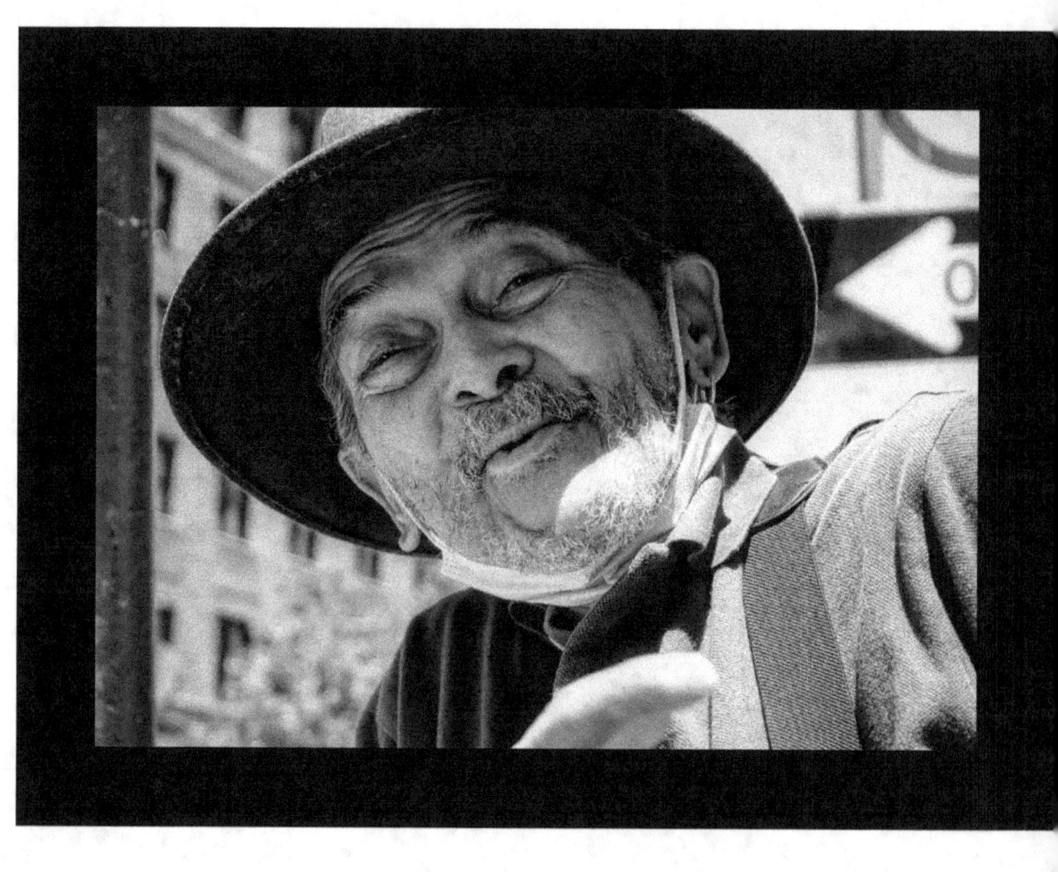

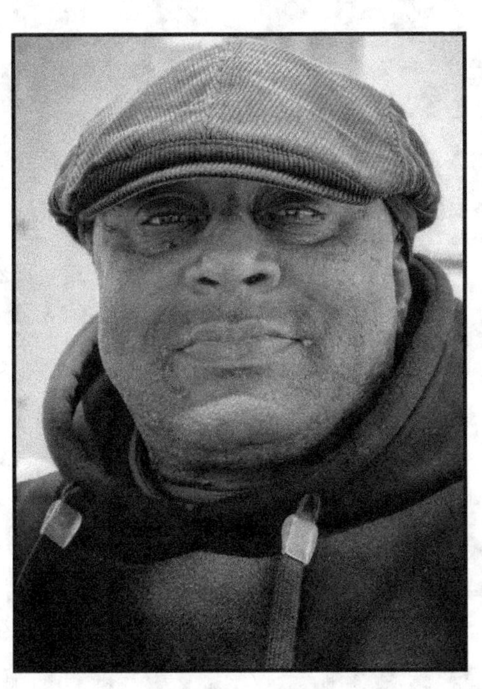 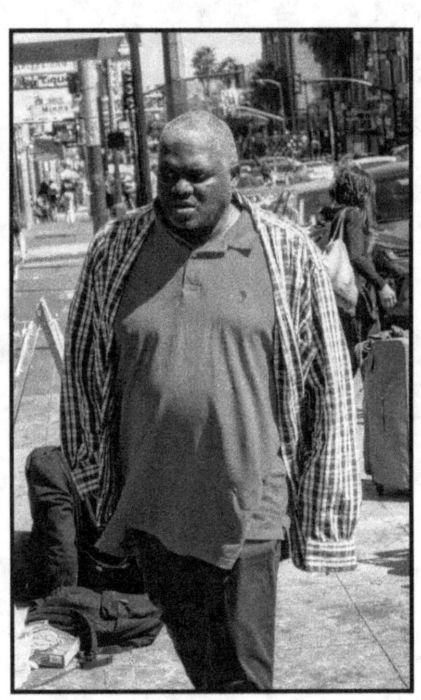

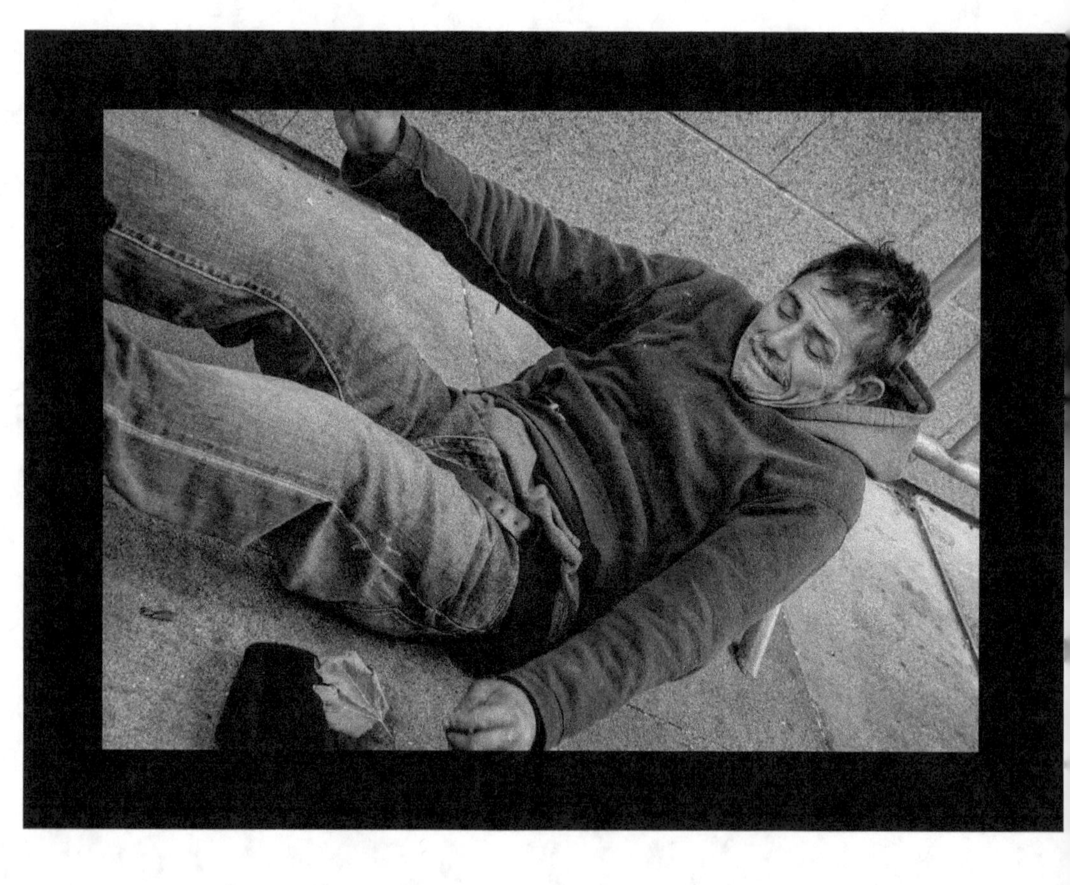

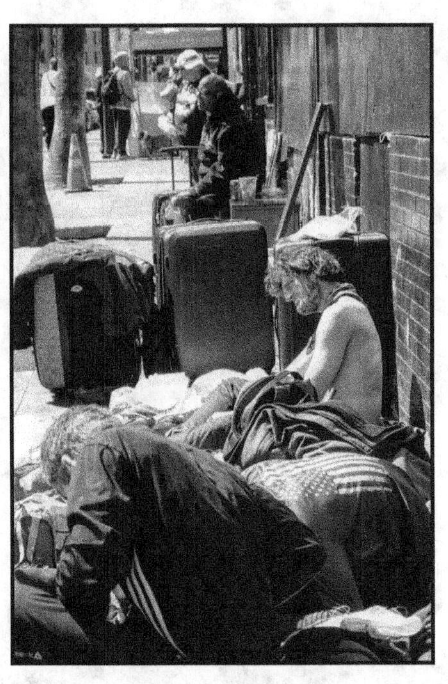 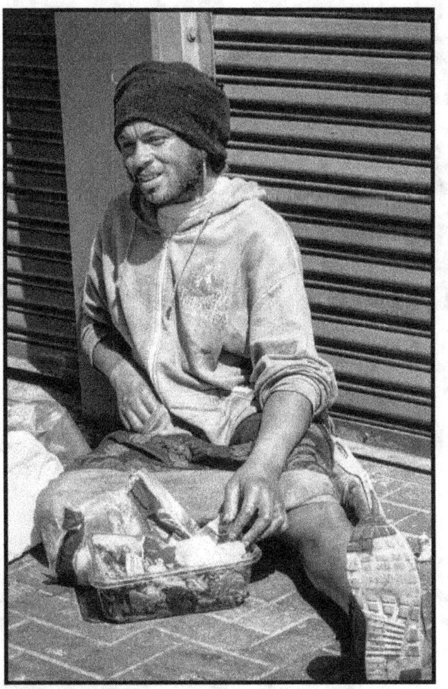

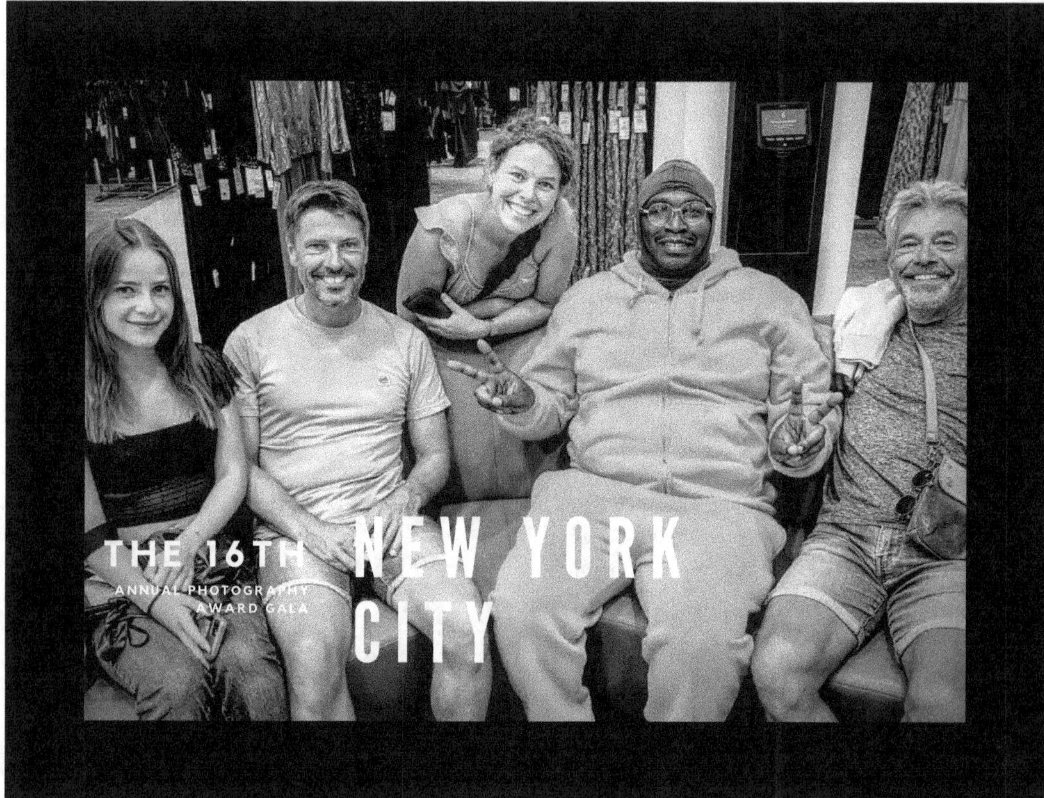
THE 16TH NEW YORK
ANNUAL PHOTOGRAPHY CITY
AWARD GALA

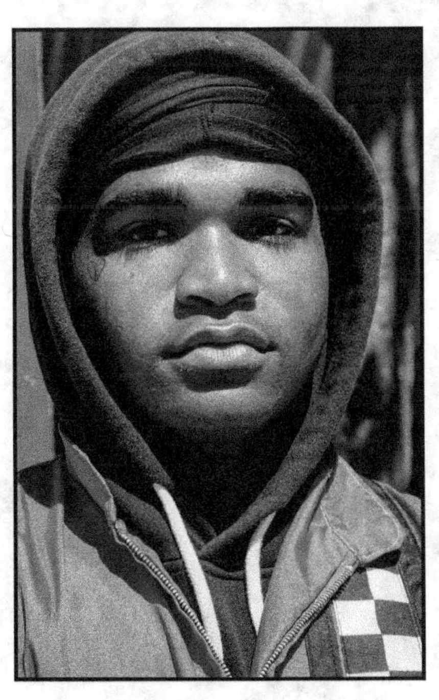
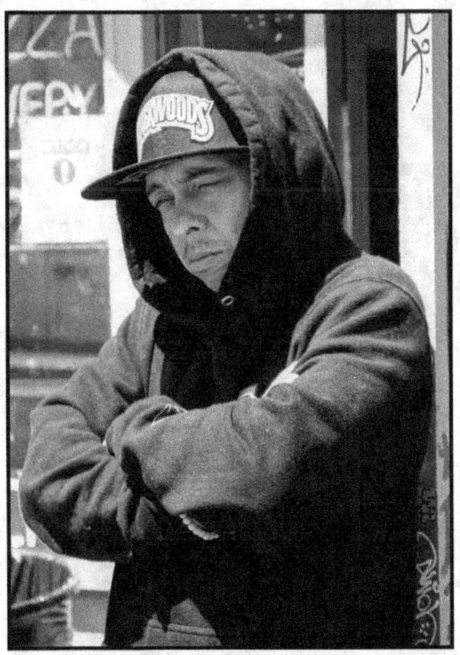

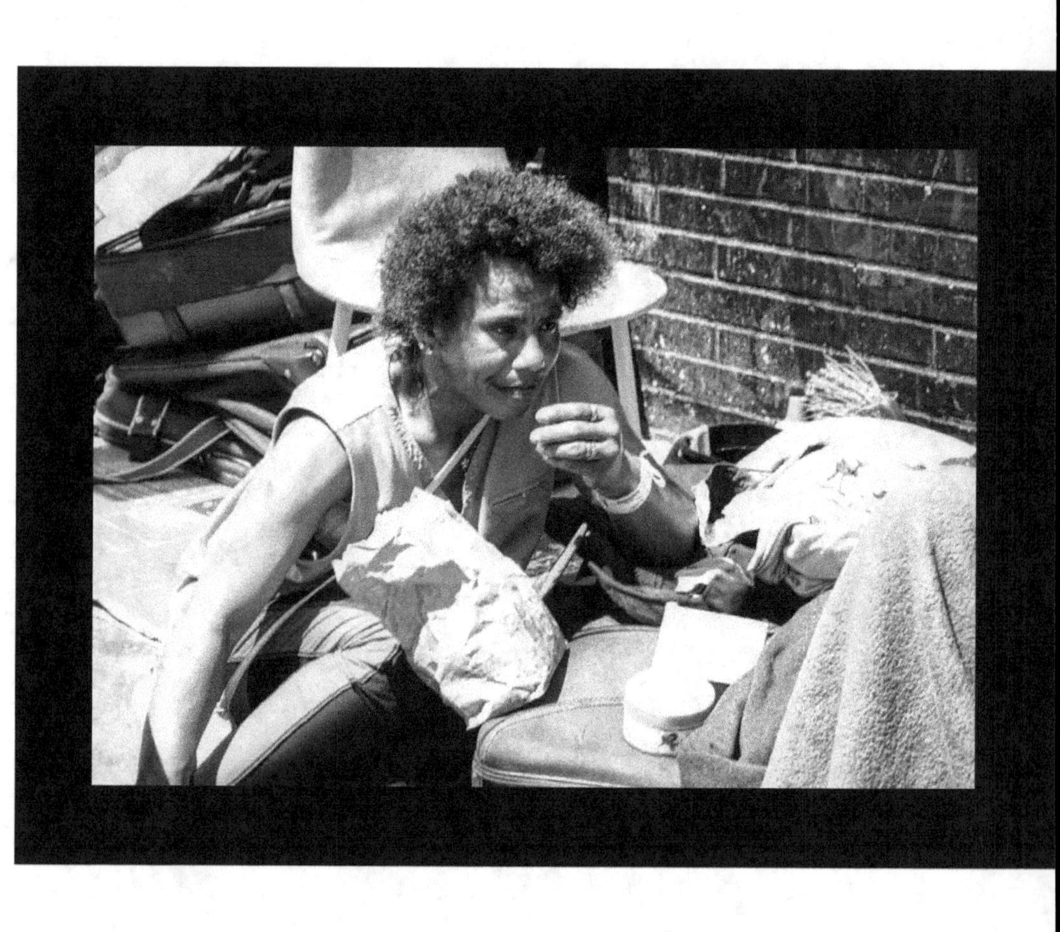

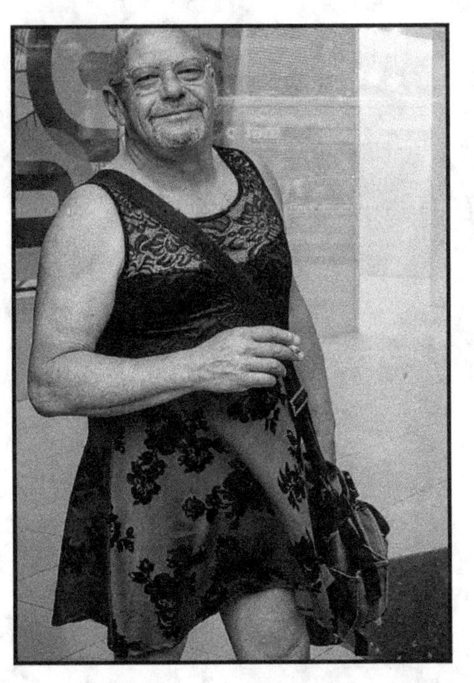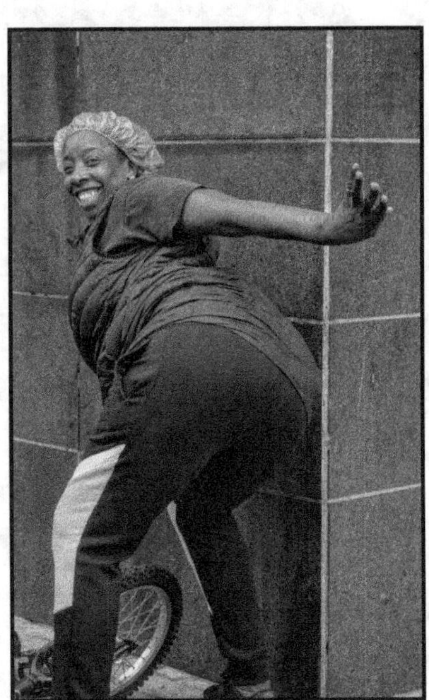

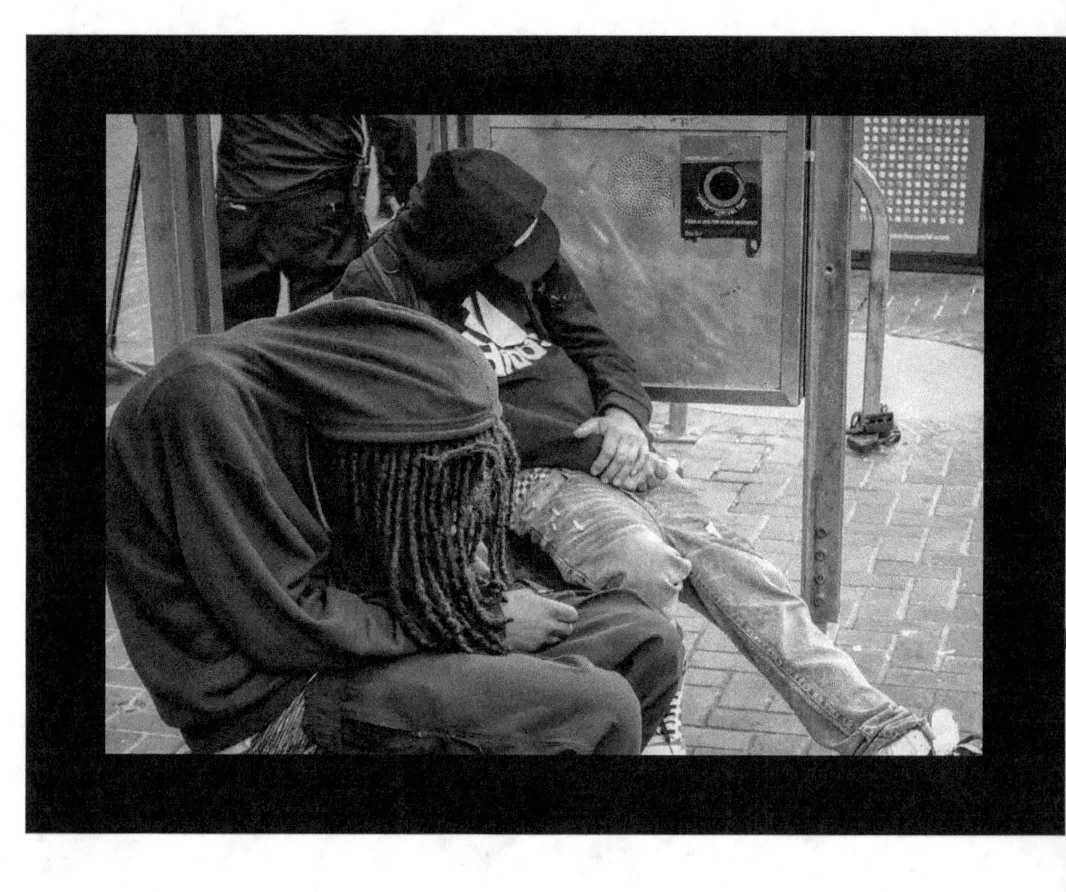

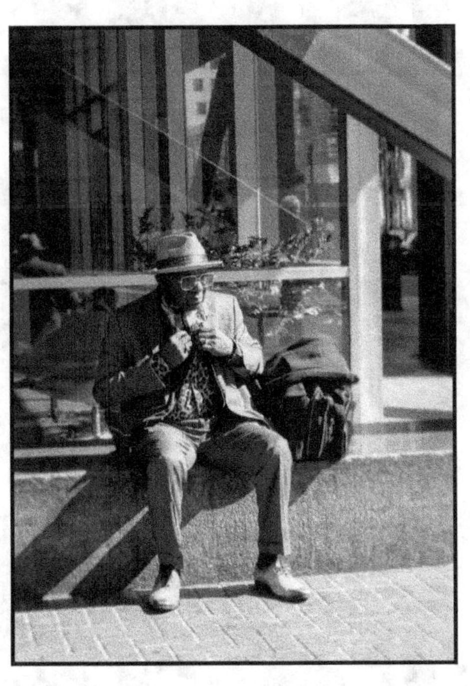

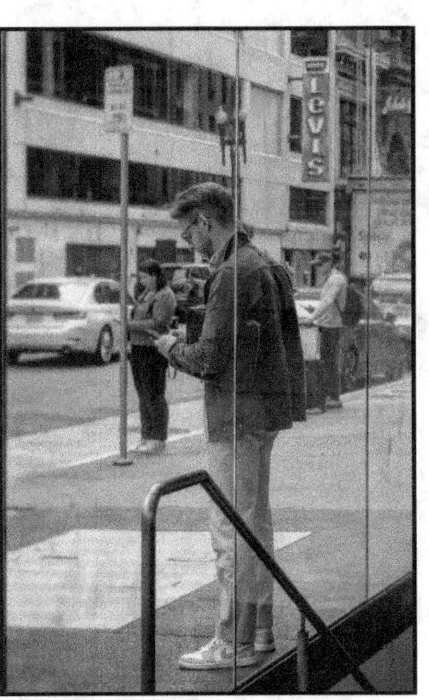

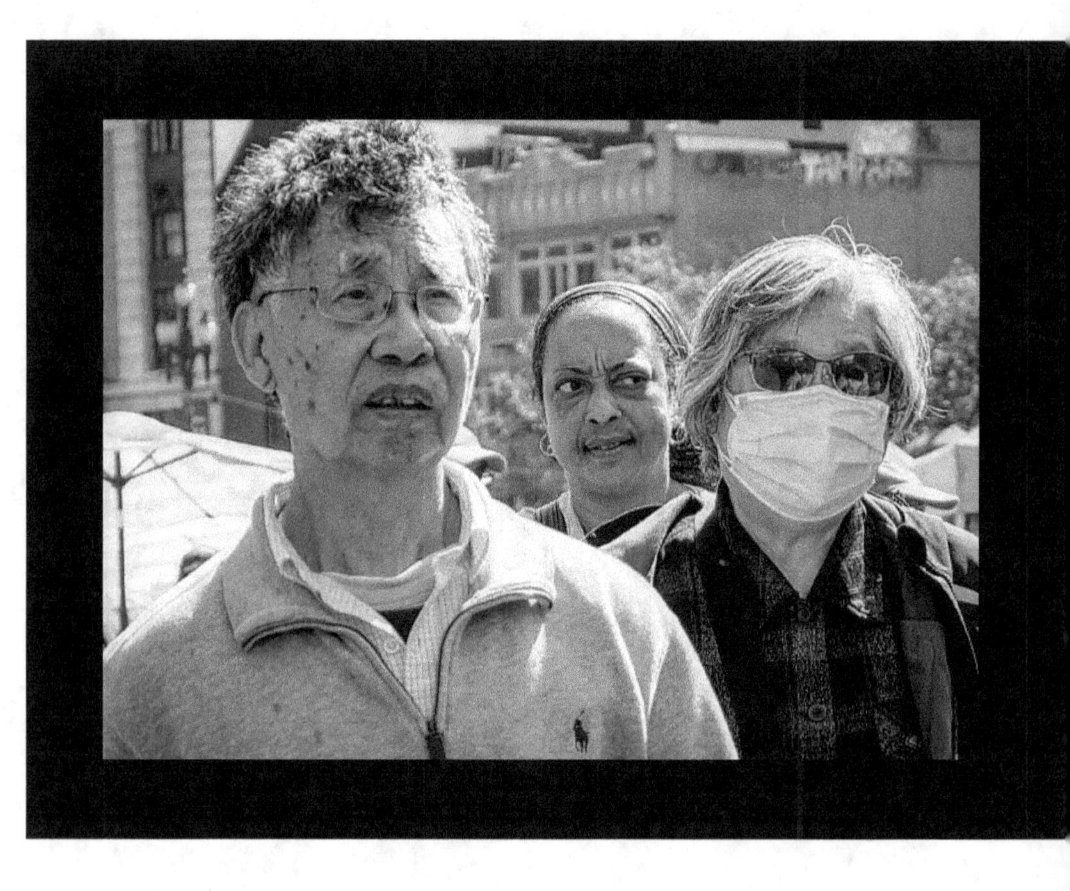

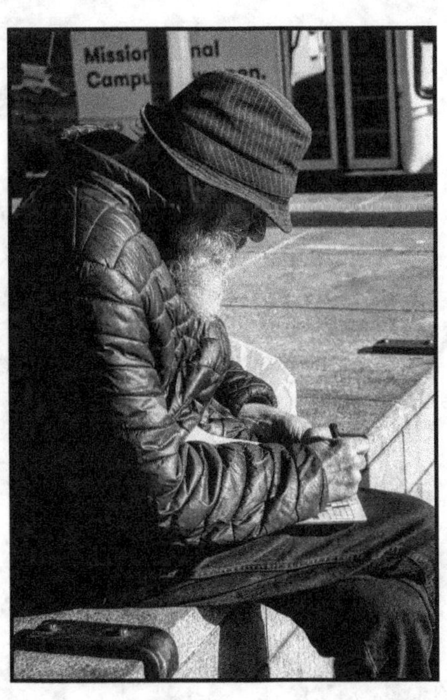
Mission nal
Campu en.

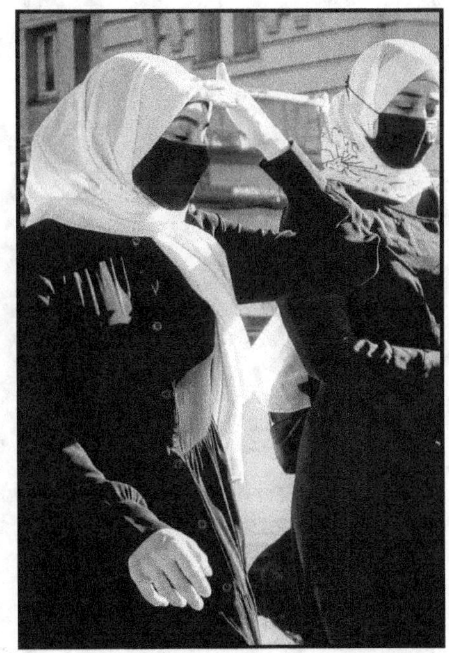

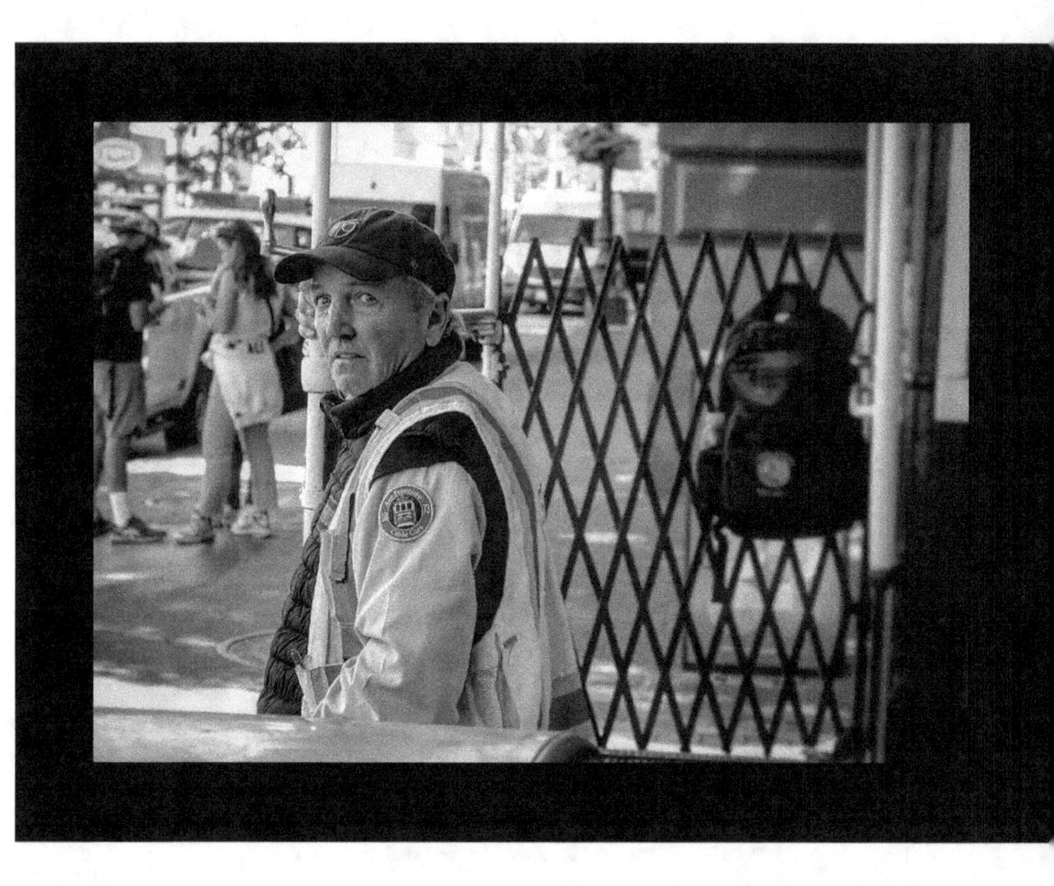

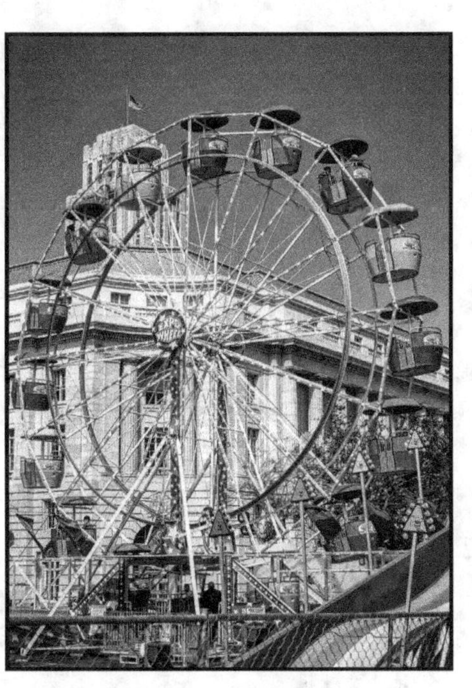
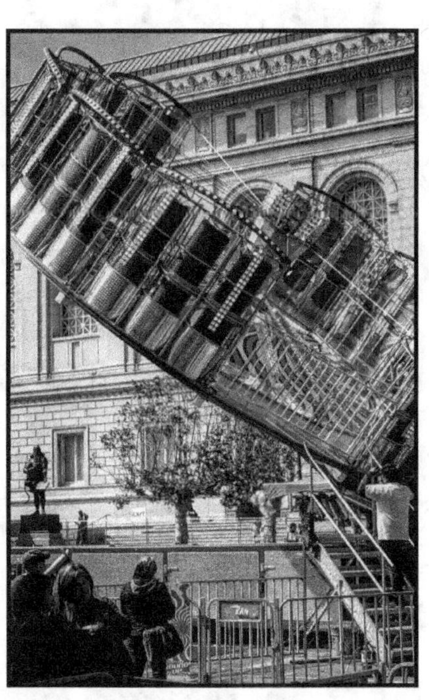

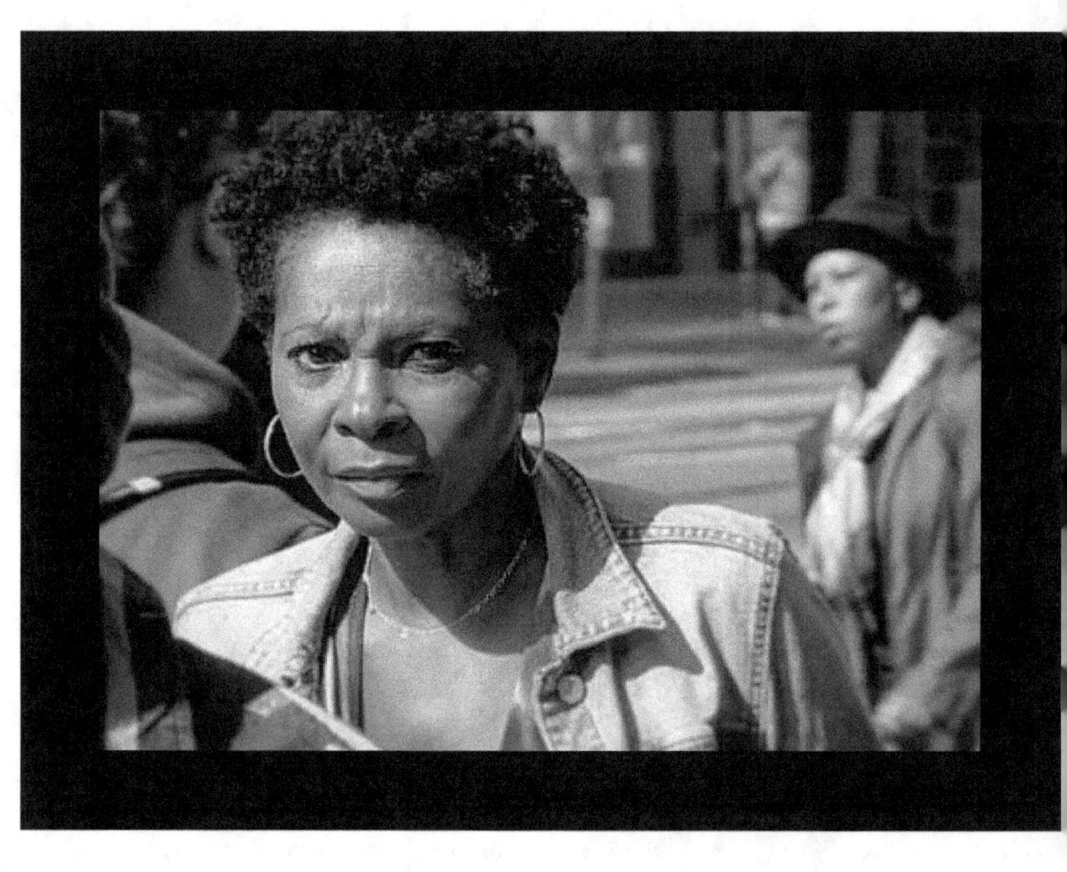

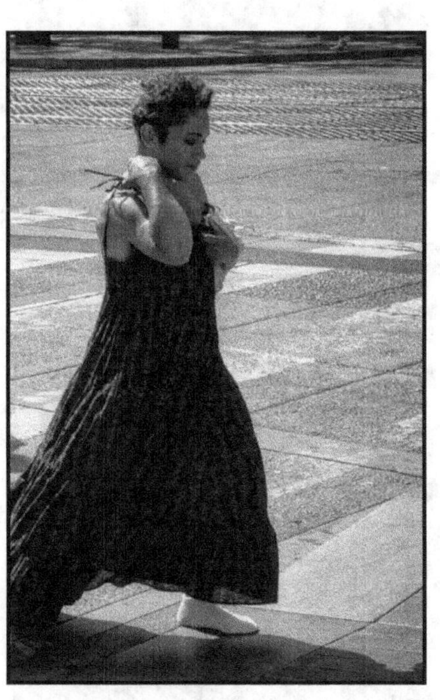
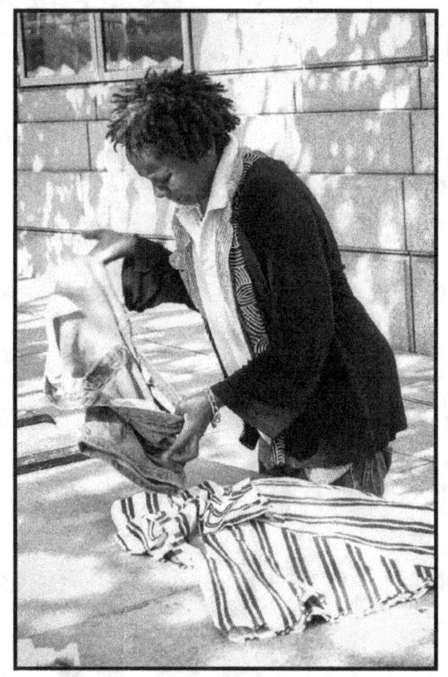

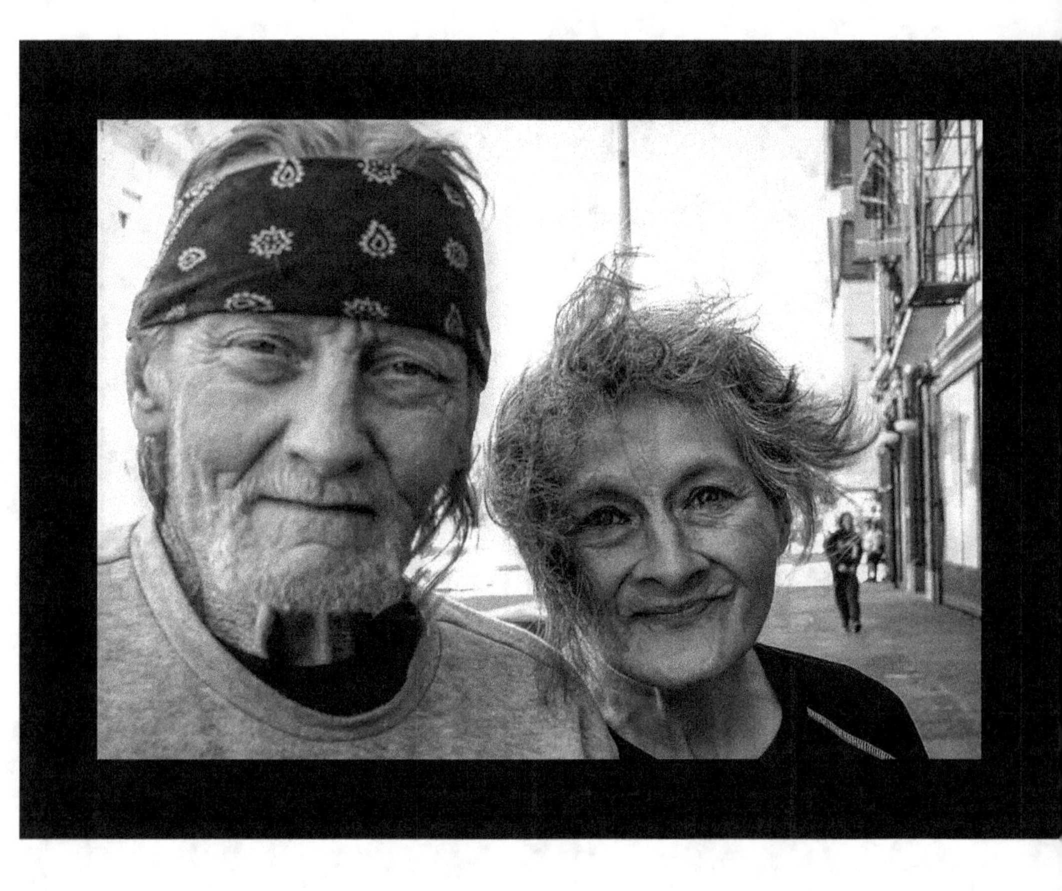

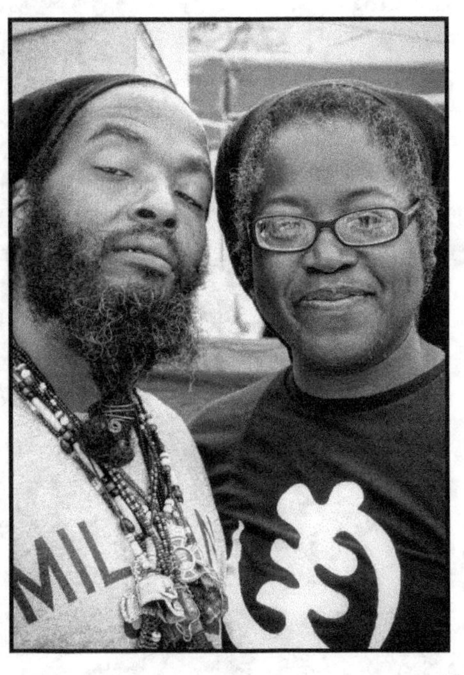
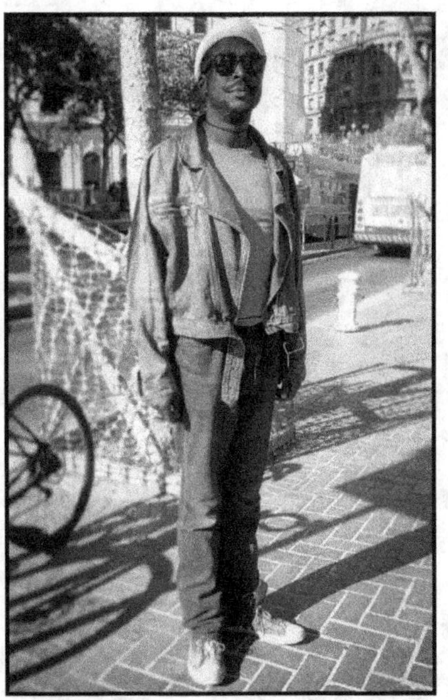

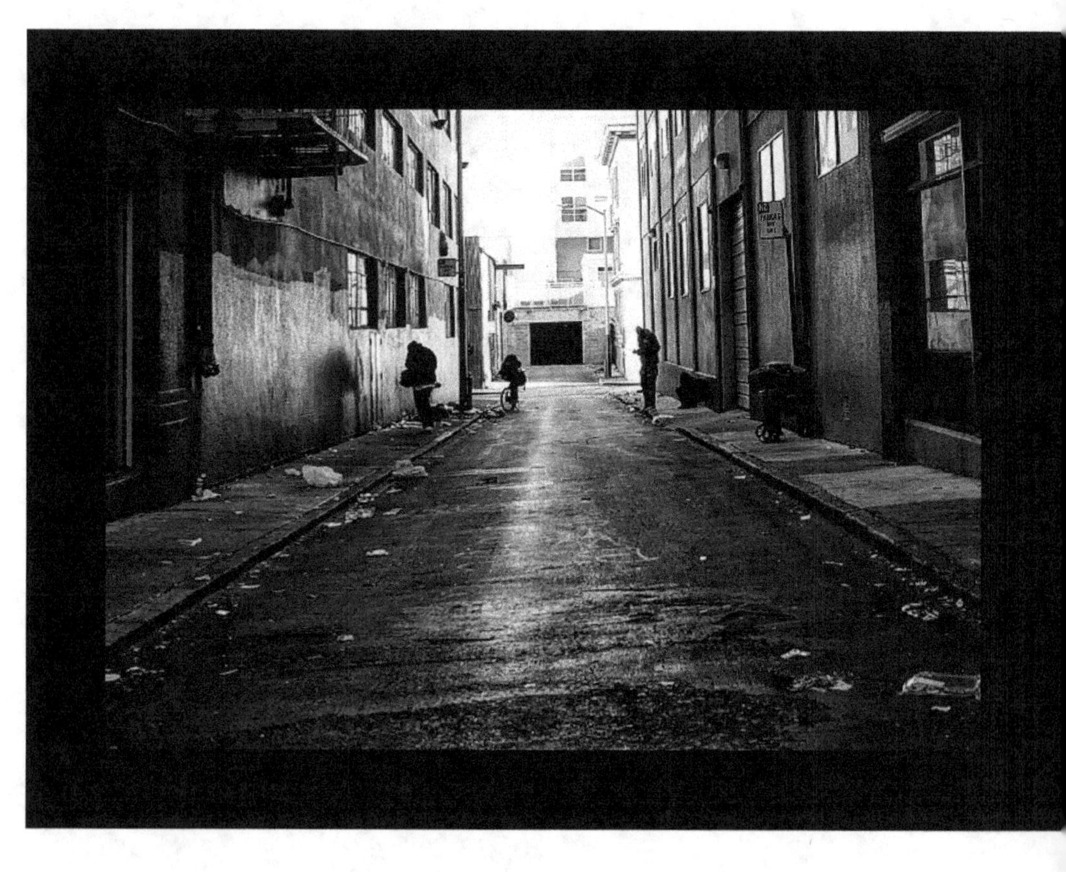

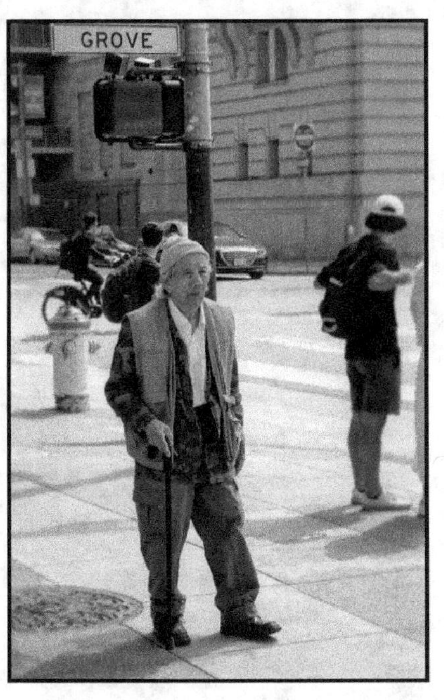
GROVE

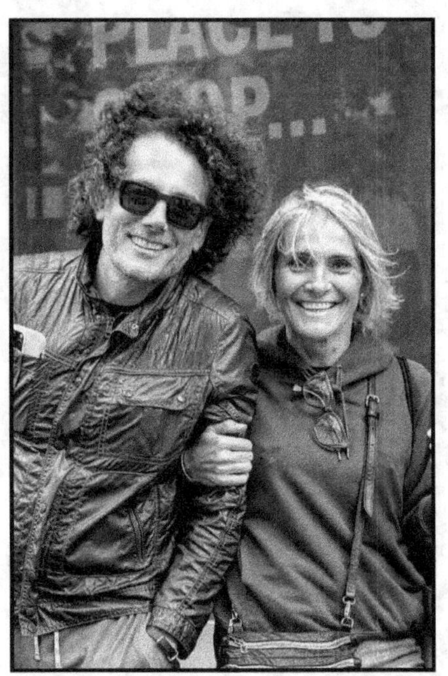
PLACE TO
SHOP...

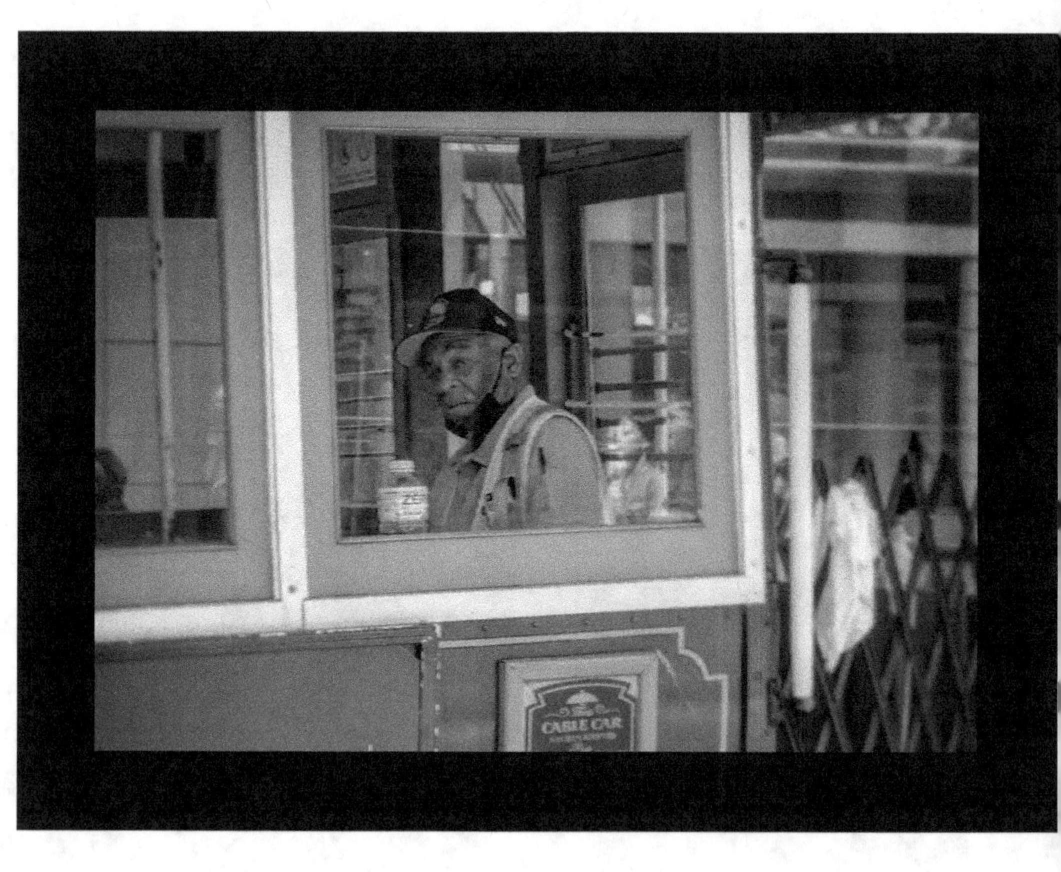

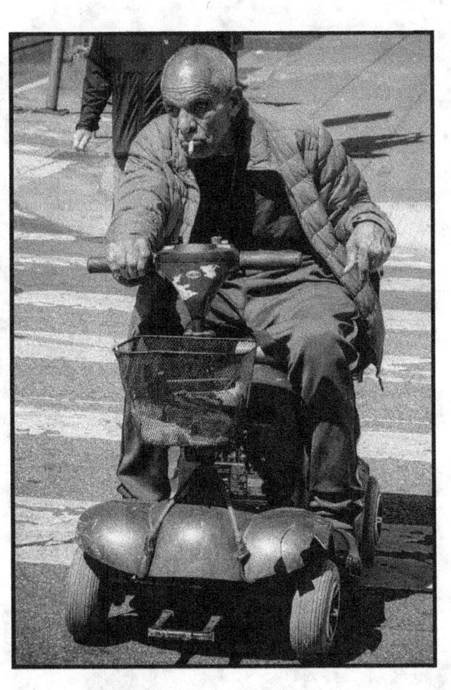 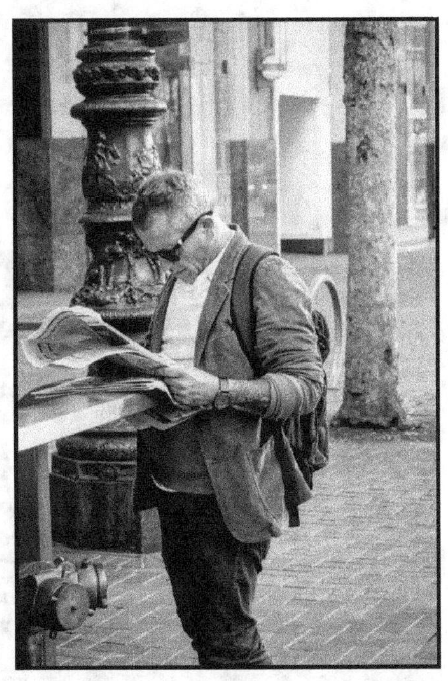

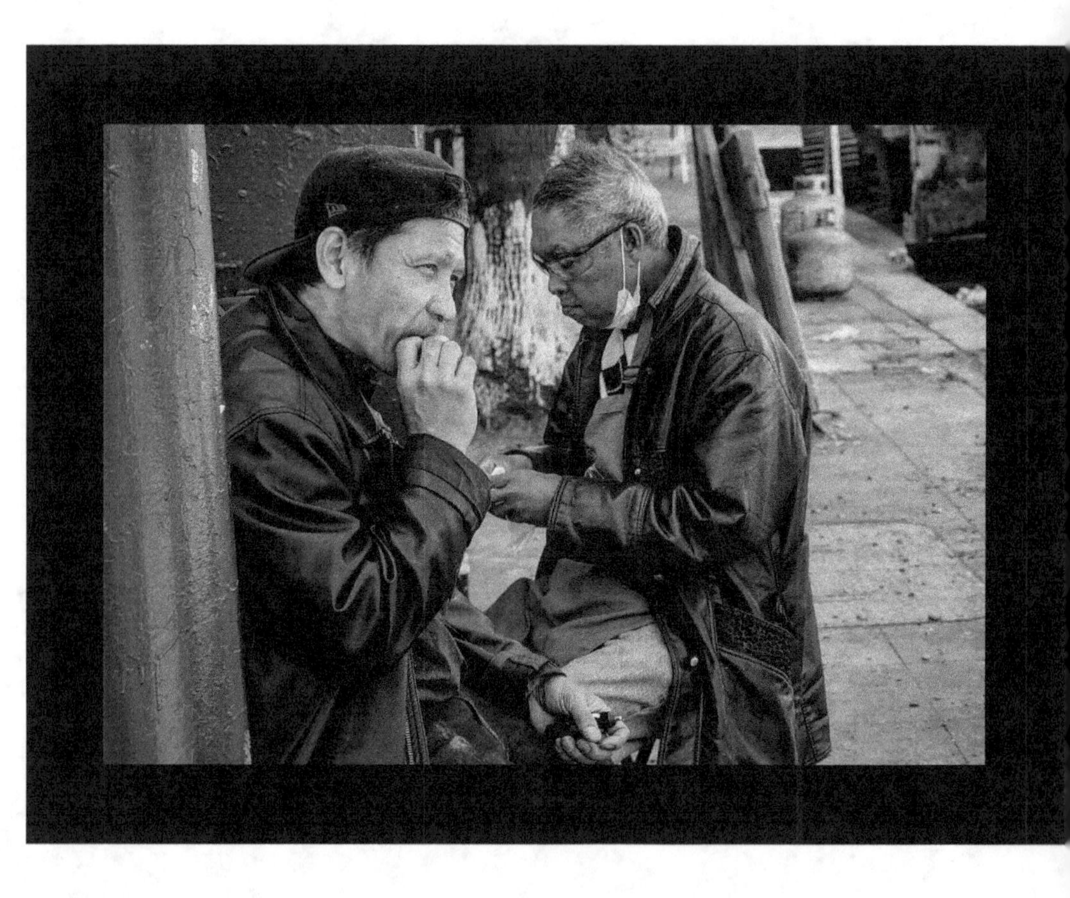

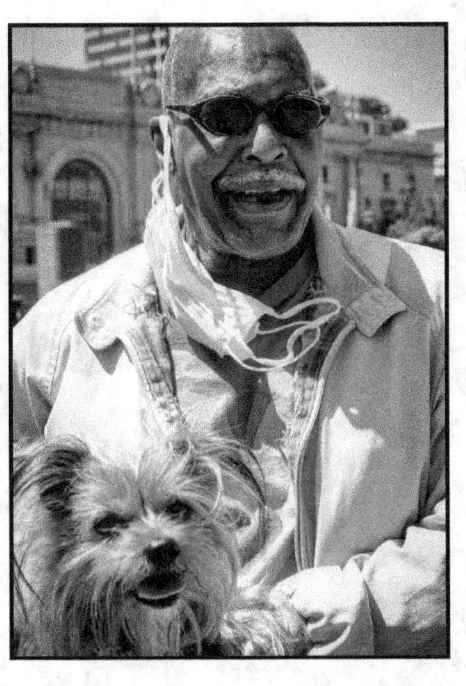 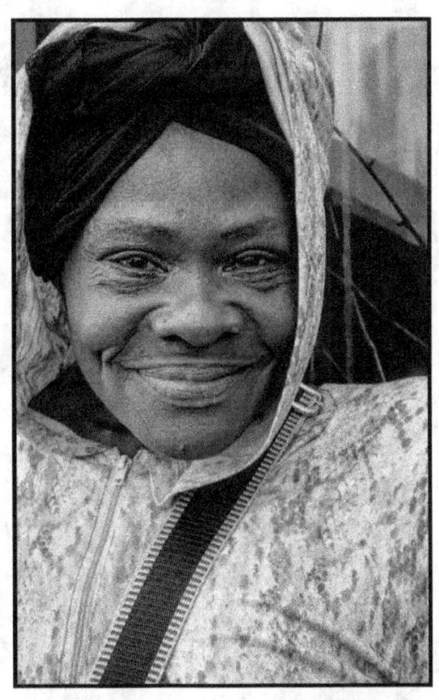

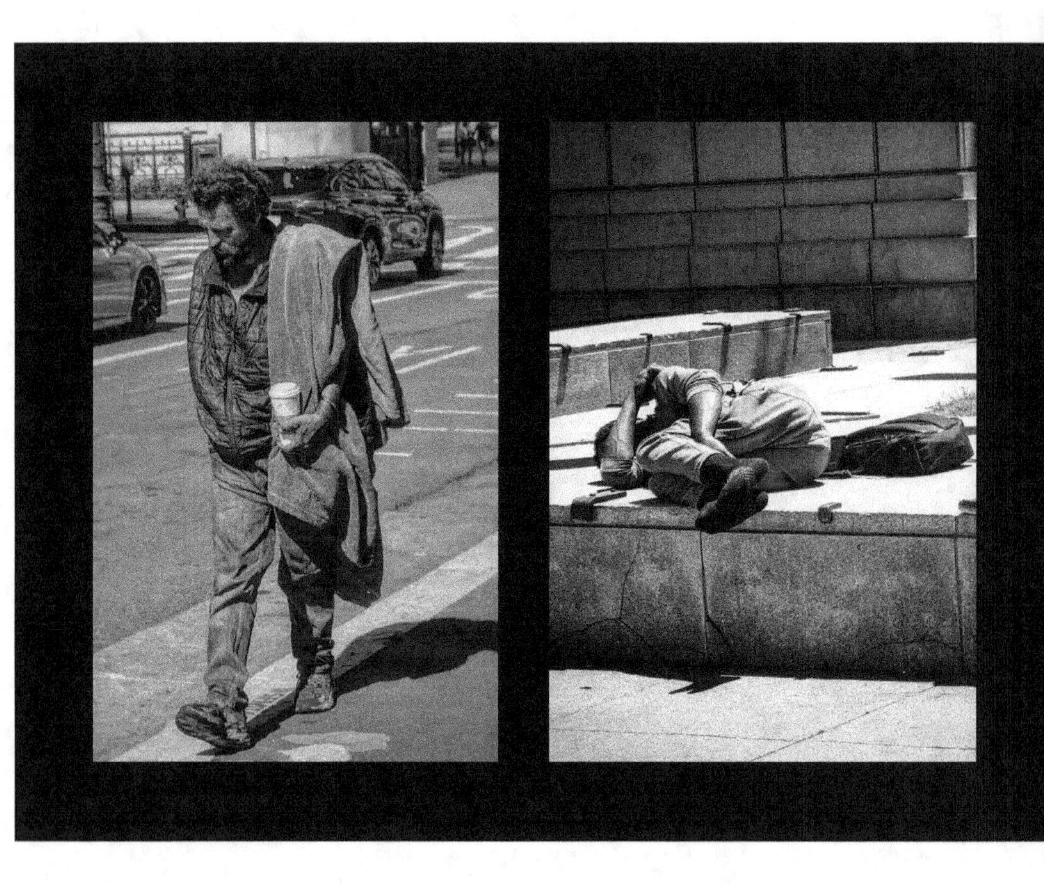

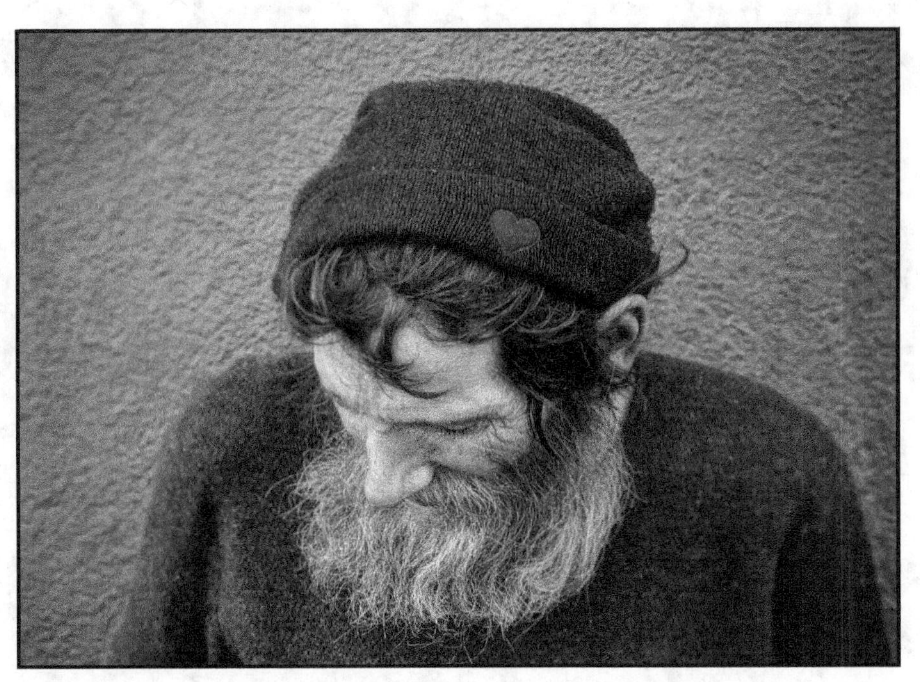

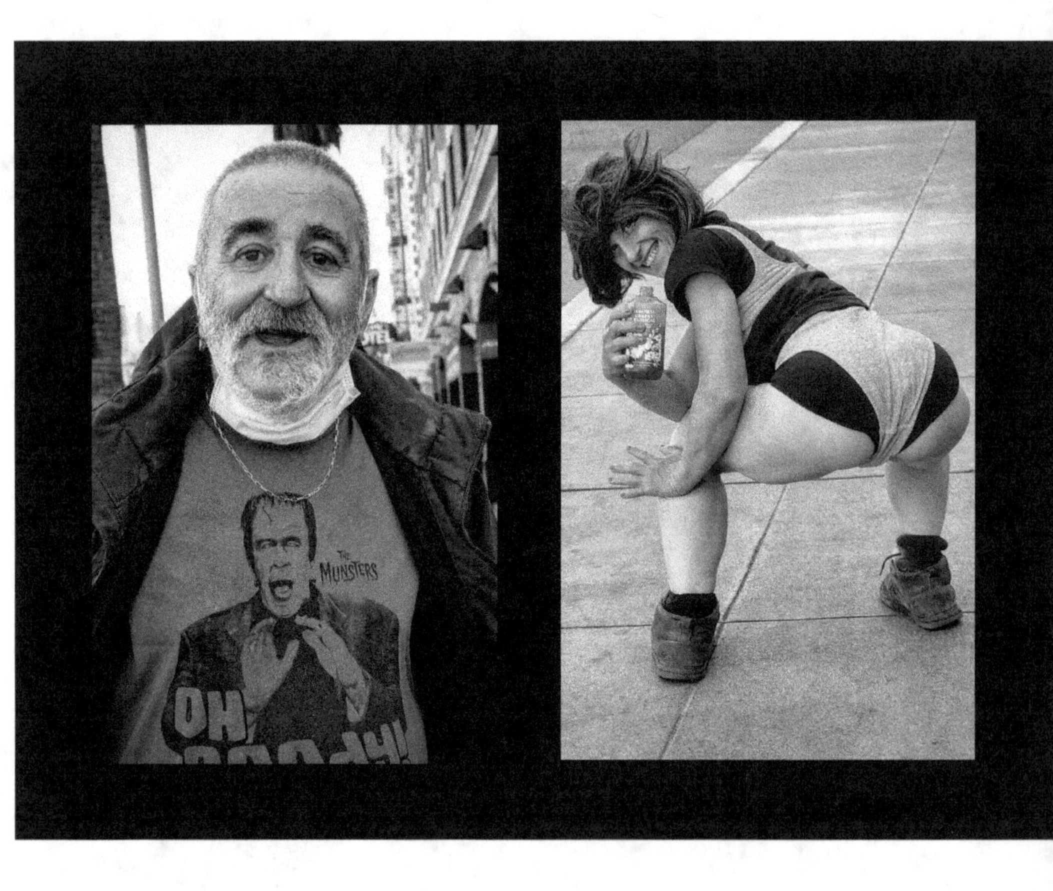

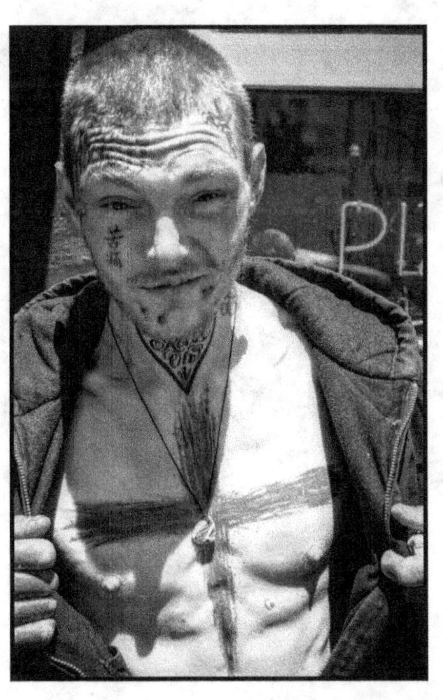
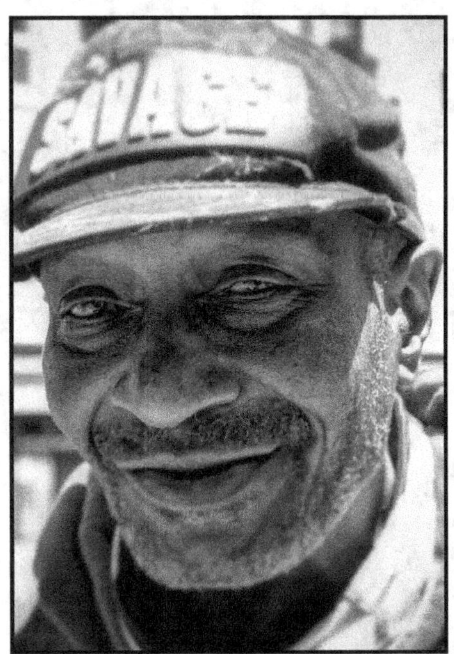

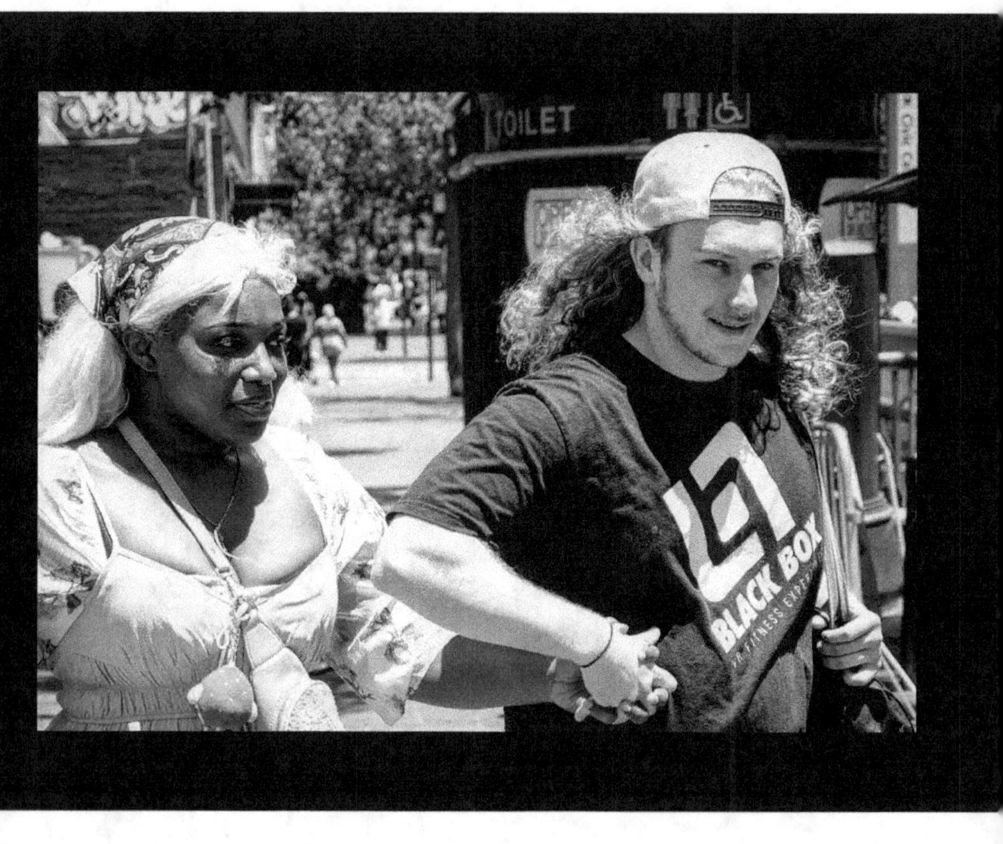
TOILET
BLACK BOX

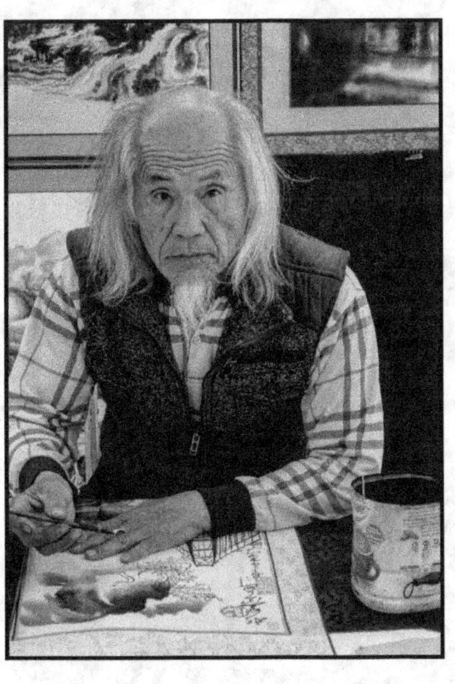
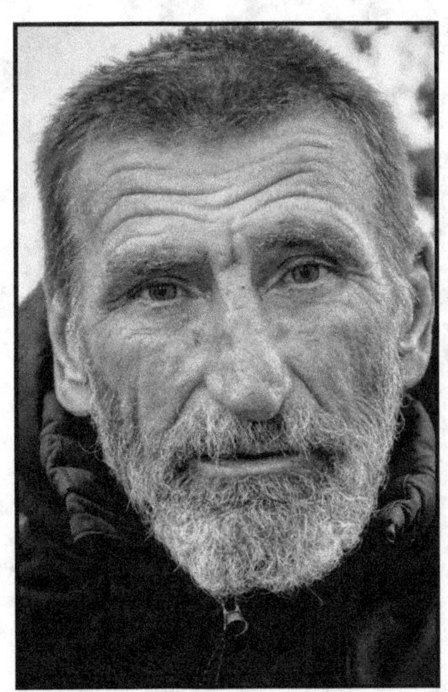

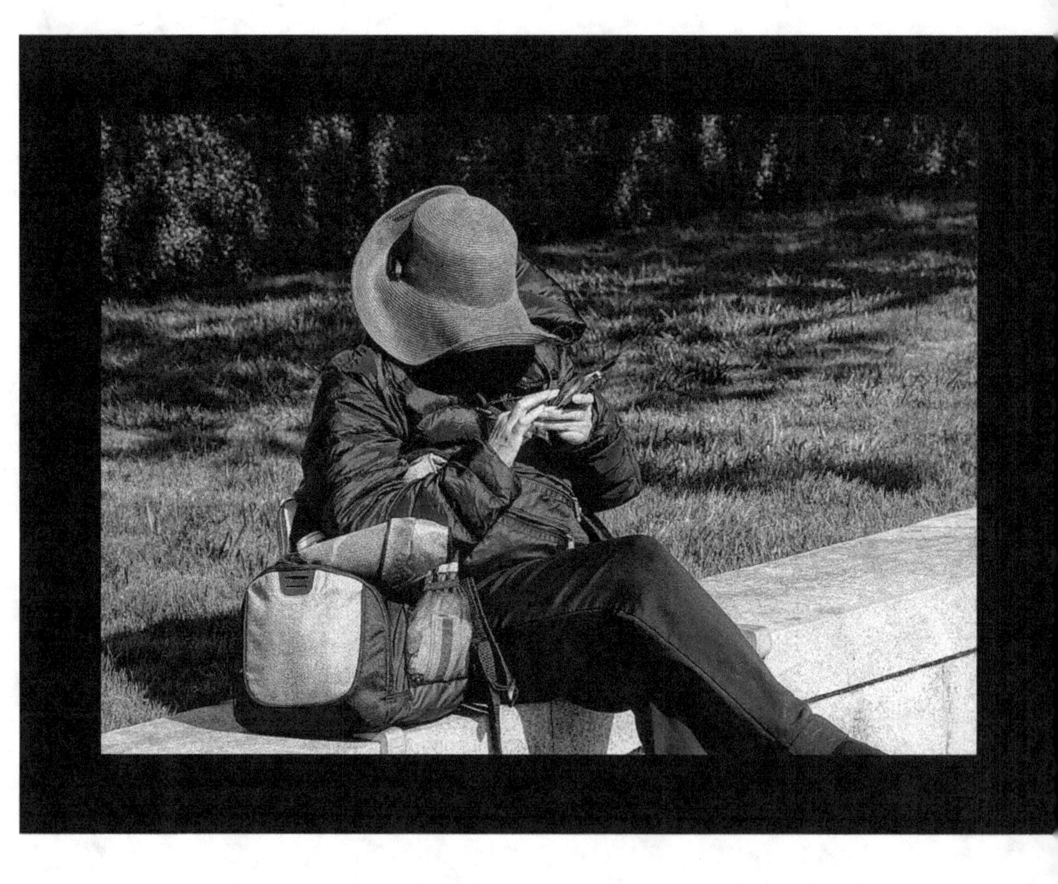

2023
THE COLLECTIVE
Award - Winning Photographer
A Vintage photo book by Donald Washington Jr.